WATERSIDE WALKS
In Hampshire

Peter Carne

COUNTRYSIDE BOOKS
NEWBURY BERKSHIRE

COUNTRYSIDE BOOKS
3 Catherine Road
Newbury, Berkshire

ISBN 1 85306 469 6

Designed by Graham Whiteman
Cover illustration by Colin Doggett
Maps by Jack Street
Photographs by the author

Produced through MRM Associates Ltd., Reading
Typeset by Acorn Bookwork, Salisbury
Printed by Woolnough Bookbinding Ltd., Irthlingborough

Contents

Walk

❦

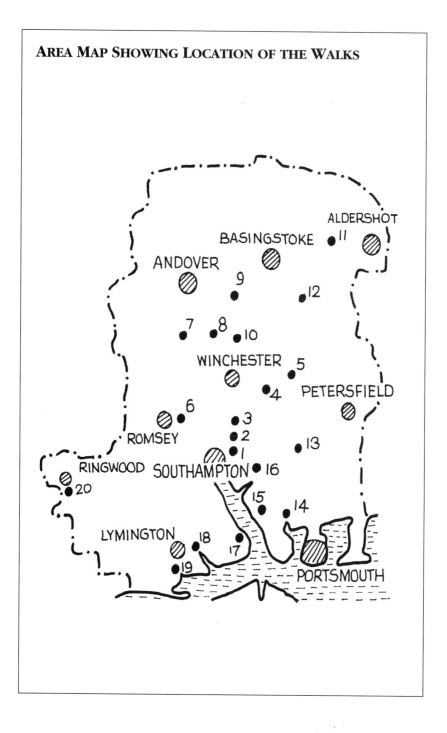

AREA MAP SHOWING LOCATION OF THE WALKS

INTRODUCTION

Water being fundamental to all life, it is hardly surprising that waterside and waterborne leisure activities exercise so strong an appeal to people of all ages. Waterside walking is one of the very best kinds of outdoor recreation, and the county of Hampshire offers a wider choice of walks close to water than almost anywhere else in England.

The routes in this book explore the valleys of famous chalk streams, the Itchen, Test and Avon, as well as those of slightly lesser-known ones – the Dever, Alre, Meon, Wey and Wallington. Towing-paths alongside old canals also make their contribution, as do footpaths beside scenic estuaries and along the shore itself. Each walk has its own very special charm, and one of the pleasures and privileges of planning this guide to watery ways ideal for leisuretime walkers was actually going over the routes and enjoying their individual attractions – not for the first time, in many instances, though I was pleased to discover some new ones I might otherwise have neglected.

Each of these circuits leaves the waterside for at least part of its route to give those who follow it the chance to sample something of the neighbouring countryside. Some of the walks bridge water or follow paths closely parallel with it rather than stick to the water's edge as such when they come into contact with it, but this variety only enhances one's enjoyment of the whole. Walkers are recommended to try as many different routes as possible and then decide which are their favourites, to be enjoyed again in the future and introduced to their friends.

None of the walks is more than about 5 miles long, and several are much shorter. All are within the capacity of the average person, including those of mature years and families with young children. Where paths with a hard surface exist, and these are mentioned in the text, normal outdoor footwear should prove adequate, but there are also some moist stretches, especially in winter or after wet weather, and the best plan, if in any doubt, is to wear stout, waterproof boots or shoes (green wellies are often my own choice!).

For your extra enjoyment and convenience, each walk either starts from or near a pub, or passes a named pub en route, so that you can refresh yourself with a drink, plus perhaps a snack or a full meal, before, during or after your outing on foot. It should be stressed, however, that details given of such places in this book are subject to change. Telephone numbers are included in case you want to make enquiries in advance of your visit. There is also information about the parking facilities available, at pubs and otherwise. Walkers should always obtain permission from pub landlords before leaving their cars in pub car parks while they are actually walking. For those readers who may lack their own transport or who wish to leave their cars at home, details of the availability of buses and trains are given for each walk. The telephone number to ring for all train service enquiries is 01345 484950. A list of the relevant bus companies and their telephone numbers is given at the end of the book.

I am indebted to my friend and fellow walking enthusiast Jack Street, author of *Pub Walks near Bournemouth and Poole*, another Countryside Books publication, for drawing the sketch maps which accompany each walk. It should be emphasised that these are intended to be no more than sketch maps, are not to scale and are provided to identify the starting point and general direction taken by each route. The Ordnance Survey Pathfinder maps, or Outdoor Leisure series where available, both on a scale of 1:25 000, are especially designed for walkers. Readers are urged to equip themselves with the relevant map, or maps, for each walk, details of which are given in the text.

Always observe the Countryside Code – remember to close all gates behind you, to keep your dog on a lead where vulnerable wildlife or farm livestock are at risk and, especially, not to leave litter or otherwise mar other people's enjoyment or rightful use of the ground where you walk. All the routes incorporate public rights of way. Our legal right to enjoy these in no way lessens the importance of always doing all we can to help make walkers welcome everywhere.

I wish you happy waterside walking in some of the loveliest corners of Hampshire.

Peter Carne

WALK 1

SOUTHAMPTON AND THE ITCHEN VALLEY COUNTRY PARK

Some of Hampshire's loveliest waterside walks are surprisingly close to towns. A full-bodied river, an old canal, a stretch of long distance path and a scenic country park mingle their many charms to delight you during this ramble on the outskirts of Southampton.

The River Itchen where it follows a winding course through ancient water-meadows many of which now form part of Itchen Valley Country Park

Your walk begins at the White Swan, a well-known hostelry sandwiched between the busy A27 and a particularly delightful stretch of the Itchen east of Swaythling. From a riverside patio and rear garden you can watch ducks and other water-loving birds while sampling, say, a pint of Ruddles County, Theakstons Best or John Smith's Bitter, perhaps by way of whetting your appetite for a succulent roast from the carvery for which this

8

Scottish and Newcastle owned restaurant and tavern has acquired a special reputation.

Inside the pub you can relax in a truly friendly, welcoming atmosphere. The White Swan is famous for its carvery where turkey and beef are always available, together with either pork or gammon. Traditional pub food such as pies, ploughman's, jacket potatoes and rolls is also available from the bar menu. There is tempting children's food – and an outside play area for the younger generation. Weekday opening times are 11 am to 11 pm and on Sundays the White Swan is at your service from midday until 10.30 pm. The restaurant, for which it is always wise to book, is open from 12 noon to 2 pm and 6 pm to 9.30 pm (10.30 pm on Saturdays).

Telephone: 01703 473322.

- **HOW TO GET THERE:** The White Swan is situated just outside Southampton proper, on the north side of the A27, on your left shortly after crossing the river Itchen as you head east in the Fareham and Portsmouth direction from Swaythling. Both Southampton Citybuses and Solent Blue buses serve the area.
- **PARKING:** As well as the White Swan's own car park, limited parking space is available on the adjacent service road, alongside the river.
- **LENGTH OF THE WALK:** 3½ miles. Map: OS Outdoor Leisure 22 New Forest (GR 450156).

THE WALK

From the White Swan walk west along the riverside service road, with the Itchen directly to your right and trees screening the A27 on your left. Where the service road ends a metalled path leads on under the A27 river bridge to much older Mansbridge, now a pedestrian crossing-point only, immediately beyond. From Mansbridge you will be following part of the Itchen Way, a waymarked route which runs between Southampton and the village of Hinton Ampner. Cross Mansbridge and double back right-handed under the A27 along another metalled path, signposted 'Public footpath, Winchester 12'.

Just beyond the bridge, where the metalled path bends left, follow a green path ahead, with the river at first on your right and then the old Itchen Navigation, a canalised side-channel of

9

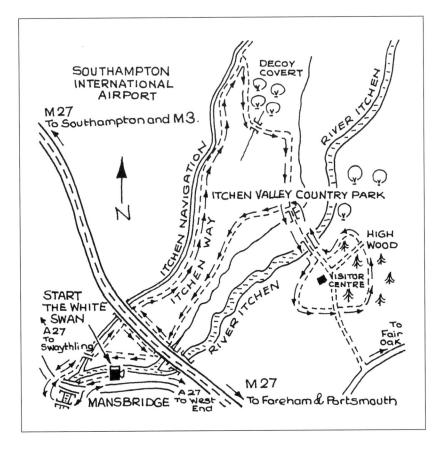

the Itchen. This artificial waterway carried barge traffic between Southampton and Winchester until 1869, when competition from the railway forced the abandonment of this unhurried means of conveying heavy merchandise.

Your path soon converges with a tree-lined track which you follow right-handed to cross the old Navigation by a substantial wooden footbridge. You pass the remnants of an old Navigation lock as a hard-surfaced path now leads you on, between the waterway and fenced meadows, to where the M27 motorway strides across the Itchen Valley. Your path here diverges right to follow the motorway for a few hundred yards before passing under it by a bridge where an arm of the Itchen flows beside you. Beyond the bridge your path, now gravelled, turns left to follow the M27's north side back to the banks of the Navigation, from which point you follow the old towing-path where barge-horses used to labour, slowly hauling their weighty charges.

Trees overhang the Navigation's course, here mainly dry now, and shade your path as you follow it north for nearly a mile before crossing a stile on your right to enter Itchen Valley Nature Reserve, as a notice here reminds you.

Now follow a waymarked path right-handed to another stile, just to the right of a field gate. Beyond this, what waymarks identify as the Meadows Nature Trail is arrowed here as leading ahead, a direction better interpreted as following the left-hand edge of the meadow you now enter, with a wood called Decoy Covert to your left.

Where the woodland edge turns left your path turns with it to cross a minor channel of water by a wooden bridge, this being followed within yards by a wooden walkway across wet ground. Where the wood edge soon turns left again, walk slightly to the right of straight ahead to cross a narrow strip of moist ground, then head left across the greensward towards a clearly visible waymarking post some 200 yards in that direction. From there the route of your path becomes clearer, crossing bridges and culverts at intervals as you now follow it right-handed, with an Itchen sidestream to your left.

Your path briefly separates from the sidestream to follow a more direct course to a gated wooden bridge which spans the minor waterway. Cross this bridge and the pasture beyond, halfway across which you go over a wooden walkway before heading for a substantial bridge across the main river. Cross this to follow an unmetalled road uphill for a few yards, then turn right through a kissing-gate preceding Itchen Valley Country Park's waymarked Woodlands and Meadows Walk.

At the end of a tall hedge on your left, turn left through another kissing-gate to cross a meadow to a third such gate. Now go over the country park's vehicle access road and proceed through a gate straight ahead into a small paddock. A hard path soon leads left-handed to follow a sinuous course through a pinewood, in which you twice cross a separate horse-riding route. After briefly emerging into the open to cross the approach road to a large field in which is a recreational area, immediately to your right here, the waymarked walk coincides briefly with a separate Forest Trail as it leads you left-handed through more woodland. Where the Forest Trail soon turns right, the Woodlands and Meadows Walk leads ahead to end at the country park's Visitor Centre.

Open daily between 11 am and teatime from April to September and at weekends during the winter half of the year, the Centre highlights local wildlife interest and other features of the park, which is owned by the Borough of Eastleigh and safeguards over 400 precious acres of unspoilt countryside. There are outdoor tables and seating for picnickers, and café facilities are available. Summer barbecues are held here.

A broad Itchen Valley panorama unfolds invitingly as you now follow the road that leads downhill and back across the main river Itchen. Recross the meadow and the wooden bridge beyond this, then immediately turn left to rejoin the Meadows Nature Trail.

This follows an Itchen sidestream, soon bridging one of the many 'carriers' which once channelled water to where it was most needed when the meadows were flooded each spring to stimulate earlier growth of grass. Next is a wooden walkway, beyond which the sidestream and path follow slightly separate courses as you approach and cross a trackway which runs at right-angles to your path. Beyond the next footbridge the nature trial takes a right-hand turn across hawthorn-studded pastures, but you continue ahead, bearing slightly left to where a waymarking post marks a gap in a straggly hedgerow. After passing through this your path rejoins the sidestream you last followed, leading you to a stile beyond which you pass back under the motorway.

Now cross a stile directly ahead to follow a field path to another stile, beyond which you turn right along the right-hand edge of a meadow. When you pass another stile on your right the field path angles slightly left to cross a footbridge preceding the next small meadow. Beyond this you pass through a gap in a hedge and cross a stile to rejoin close to an old Navigation lock the surfaced path you followed much earlier, on the outward stage of this walk. It now leads you left-handed, back over the wooden footbridge which spans the old waterway. Beyond this you turn left for Mansbridge, the White Swan and the end of your walk.

THE ITCHEN AT BISHOPSTOKE
✨

Waterside walkers are spoilt for choice along the peaceful Itchen Valley. Here is another 'close to town' route you will be glad not to have missed from the very moment you start exploring it, with a splendid path alongside the old Itchen Navigation followed by a return over wide meadows close to the river itself.

The Barge public house at Bishopstoke

Bishopstoke, as its name suggests, has had strong links with the Church, having been for centuries one of the properties of the bishops of Winchester. From a quiet rural backwater it has grown, in recent decades, into a populous suburb of Eastleigh, a town which did not exist until the coming of the railway.

Side-channels of the Itchen pass close to a Whitbread pub called the Barge, well placed to serve you with refreshment before or after the waterside walk and open from 11 am to 11 pm on weekdays. Sunday hours are sometimes extended from the usual 12 noon to 3 pm and 7 pm to 10.30 pm to offer all-day opening. The Barge is large and comfortable and there is a comprehensive menu, embracing 'everything from sandwiches to steaks' and including roasts on Sunday. Food is available between 12 noon and 2.30 pm every day and from 7 pm to 9.30 pm on Wednesday to Saturday inclusive, and is all freshly cooked on the premises, with blackboard specials changing daily. Boddingtons and Ringwood real ales are complemented by guest ales, with a good range of lagers, bottled beers and wines.

Telephone 01703 612544 (booking for Sunday lunch is advisable).

- **HOW TO GET THERE:** The Barge is on the north side of the B3037 between Eastleigh and Fair Oak, ½ mile from Eastleigh.

  Trains to Eastleigh from Southampton, Winchester, Portsmouth and Fareham are frequent and Solent Blue buses also serve the area.
- **PARKING:** Besides the large car park at the Barge, a free public car park is available by a large sports ground on the Eastleigh side of Bishopstoke.
- **LENGTH OF THE WALK:** 5 miles. Maps: OS Pathfinder 1264 Winchester (South) and Eastleigh (GR 464192).

THE WALK

From the Barge head west along the road towards Eastleigh for a very short distance before bridging the Itchen Navigation, more commonly known by locals as 'The Barge', hence the name of the pub. Now turn right to follow a macadamised waterside path, part of the Itchen Way with trees overhanging the clear current of the rippling channel to your right.

Ignore a path which soon turns right to bridge 'The Barge', which remains on your right as you head north, at first with playing fields to your left, followed by meadows as you carry on through quiet countryside. Your path becomes gravelled and bridges sidestreams more than once before bending right to cross the Navigation, the tree-shaded east bank of which you now follow, presently veering slightly left to pass under the London–Southampton railway by a rather low brick arch.

Back gardens of Allbrook's houses slope down to the waterway on your left as your path follows it along a steady right-hand curve before once again passing under the railway whose arrival in 1839 sounded the Navigation's death knell. A few yards

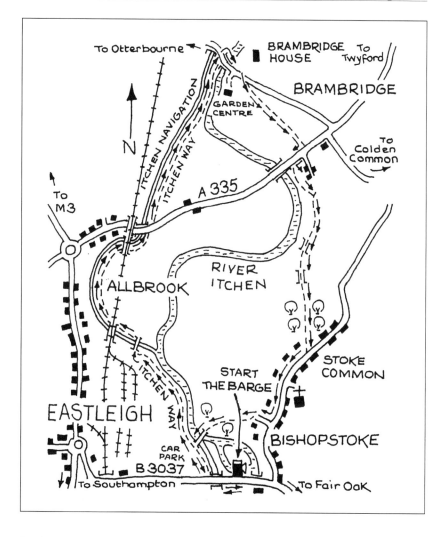

farther on you reach and cross the Eastleigh–Twyford road, the A335, then continue north past a triple weir, with the Navigation still to your left. I have seen swans, wild ducks and a water-vole here – wildlife is always worth watching out for as you enjoy these waterside walks.

Presently a river channel flanks your path on the right, and you continue with flowing water on both sides – and sometimes through culverts beneath your path – until you emerge onto the Otterbourne–Brambridge road, which you follow right-handed.

15

Through trees on your left you can catch a glimpse of Brambridge House, once the home of Mrs Fitzherbert whom George IV secretly married although the union was never officially recognised. After bridging the easternmost arm of the Itchen and passing the entrance to a garden centre you go through a kissing-gate on your right to follow a signposted footpath parallel with the right-hand edge of the meadow you now enter. Cross a stile at the end of this meadow and then two other stiles before and after a strip of woodland preceding a third meadow, halfway along the far left edge of which another stile brings you back onto the A335.

Cross this and follow it right-handed past some cottages to the near side of a bridge spanning the main stream of the Itchen. Turn left here to follow a footpath with the back gardens of houses to your left and the river on your right. After crossing a stile this joins another path which soon becomes an unfenced farm track as you follow it across a large pasture flanked by woodland away to your left and straight ahead.

Beyond a gap in a straggly hedge a series of ill-defined tracks diverge. Follow the one that leads right-ahead to the meadow's end, where a footbridge over a stream precedes a further meadow, on the far side of which, ahead, a kissing-gate and another stream footbridge mark the start of a rising woodland path which at first angles slightly right and then is stepped at steeper points. A left-hand fence flanks the final stretch of this path, which at Stoke Common joins a road that you follow right-handed back into Bishopstoke. Continue on Church Road to Oakbank Road, a short cul-de-sac which leads you right-handed to a macadamised path through trees and alongside the Itchen Navigation. Soon crossing this by a bridge, you rejoin and follow left-handed back to Bishopstoke Road and the start of your walk the path along which you first set out. The Barge pub now lies to your left and the public car park to your right.

WALK 3

THE ITCHEN VALLEY AT SHAWFORD

Here is an Itchen Valley scene which still waits to be immortalised by the brush of some famous painter. Bring your easel if you like, but at all costs do not miss this short but unforgettable outing.

The Bridge Hotel at Shawford

If landscape painter Constable had lived in Hampshire instead of in Suffolk, he would surely have chosen as one of his subjects the pastoral easterly view from Shawford, focused upon the gentle rise of Twyford church in the middle distance. Whether viewed from the same level as the Itchen or from the modest elevation of Shawford Down, just to the west, here is one of those rural panoramas that stay forever in the memory.

This is a part of the Itchen Valley where the chalk which cradles the river crowds in quite closely on both sides, emphasising by its proximity the verdant smoothness of the river-segmented levels in between. The river proper shares its water with the Itchen Navigation, here in full flow where it bounds the garden of the Bridge Hotel at Shawford, as happily situated a hostelry for waterside walkers as could be wished for. Owned by Surrey Free Inns, the white-fronted pub alongside the B3386 only yards from Shawford station offers a range of popular brews including Courage Best and Directors, John Smith's, Ruddles County and No Name Best Bitter, brewed in Priors Dean, near Petersfield. With its panelled walls and snug alcoves, the sizeable lounge bar is a well-balanced blend of style and comfort, and there is also a separate public bar. Food is served seven days a week from 12 noon to 2 pm at lunchtime and 6.30 pm to 9.30 pm in the evening, and blackboard specials supplement the Farmhouse Kitchen menu – you will find a good range of starters, grills, steaks and desserts as well as hot platters ranging from steak, stout and mushroom pie to Scottish salmon fillet with hollandaise sauce and vegetables of the day. The traditional Sunday roasts are very much in demand (booking advisable). As well as the waterside garden there is a children's outdoor play area. Pub opening times are 11 am (12 noon on Sundays) to 3 pm and 6 pm (6.30 pm on Sundays) to 11 pm (10.30 pm on Sundays) except in summer, when the pub is normally open all day on Saturdays and Sundays. Overnight accommodation is also available.

Telephone: 01962 713171.

- **HOW TO GET THERE:** Shawford lies 3 miles south of Winchester, on the B3386 midway between Compton Street and Twyford. If travelling on the M3, leave at junction 11 and follow the A3090 (signed 'Winchester South and West') for ½ mile to Compton Street crossroads and there turn right for Shawford.

  Trains between Winchester, Eastleigh, Fareham and Portsmouth call at Shawford and Solent Blue buses serve the area.
- **PARKING:** As well as the large rear car park at the Bridge Hotel, there is a public car park at the foot of Shawford Down, and parking space is also available on roads leading north from the B3386 on either side of Shawford railway bridge.
- **LENGTH OF THE WALK:** 2 miles. Map: OS Pathfinder 1264 Winchester (South) and Eastleigh (GR 475250).

THE WALK

Leaving the Bridge Hotel behind you on your left, cross the first bridge, over the Itchen Navigation, and then immediately turn

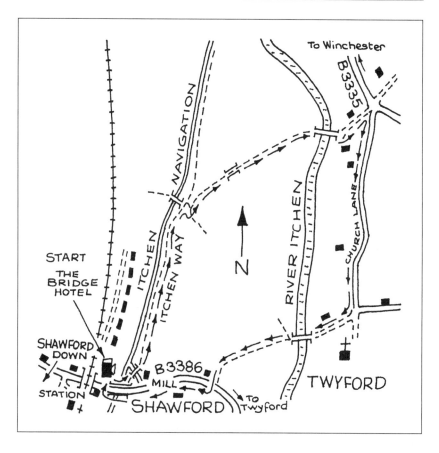

left to follow a hard path north along the Navigation's tree-shaded east bank. Soon a footbridge takes you across a sidestream leading to Shawford's old mill, to your right, then your path continues alongside the Navigation, flanked on its far side by the gardens of a series of fairly large houses. This is also part of the Itchen Way.

Pathside trees partly screen your view across watermeadows to your right until you approach within yards of another footbridge with the remains of an old Navigation lock just beyond it. Here you cross a stile on your right to follow a field path angling sharply right, then after a few yards turn left to bridge a minor side-channel and follow a path now heading north-east across watermeadows.

A boardwalk eases your way across wet ground to where a cattle-bridge over another river channel precedes a gateway, beyond which your footpath follows the right-hand edge of a further pasture to a stile at its far right corner. Cross this to follow a track ahead, soon bridging a main arm of the Itchen by an old mill to your right. Your track then climbs to the main Winchester–Botley road, having reached which you immediately bear right from it to follow Twyford's Church Lane.

A clipped yew hedge and the walled gardens of wayside dwellings in their own substantial grounds flank your approach to Twyford's church of St Mary the Virgin, which so delightfully rounds off the view from the Shawford side of the Itchen Valley. There has been a church on this site since Saxon times, and before that there may have been a Druidic temple, twelve Druid stones having been found under the tower of the Norman church demolished in 1876 to make way for the present building. This embodies the Norman arcades, a stained glass window and some other features of its predecessor.

The clipped yew in Twyford churchyard may not be quite 1,000 years old, as some have claimed, but is beyond doubt a very ancient and splendid specimen of its kind, unequalled by any other in Hampshire.

Return to where you entered the churchyard and there turn left to follow a downhill track to a gated footbridge adjoining a cattle-bridge over a mainstream of the Itchen. Cross this to enter a meadow where, after a few yards, two separate footpaths diverge. Take the path which here bears left and is slightly raised above the level of the watermeadow you now cross in a south-westerly direction. When you reach the far side of this pasture your path bends left to reach the Twyford–Shawford road, which you follow right-handed past the timbered grounds of Shawford Park mansion on your left. You bridge a side-channel of the Itchen by Shawford's old mill on your right and then soon recross the Navigation to the Bridge Hotel and your walk's end.

If time and energy permit, extend your walk west to enjoy a brief and bracing climb of Shawford Down, a county-owned open space from the top of which the Itchen Valley presents a truly spectacular panoramic view.

OVINGTON AND ITCHEN STOKE

A more peaceful village than Ovington, and a more popular or delightful riverside walk than this one to Itchen Stoke, would be very hard to find. This is a prime example of an outing you will want to enjoy not once, but many times. Your children will love it too because of the host of water-loving wildlife always on view.

The Bush Inn

Approached by narrow, tree-lined lanes and well hidden from the world outside until you actually arrive there, Ovington's records stretch back to the time when land here was granted by King Edgar to a bishop of Winchester. Of Anglo-Saxon origin, its name means 'a place above' and might equally imply 'a place apart' from the hurly-burly of modern life, so steeped in calm does it remain. Clustering cottages and farm buildings are overlooked by a 19th-century church dedicated to St Peter. Just to the north of the present steepled building stood its Norman predecessor, of which the entrance arch is all that has been preserved where it always was, although the square font was transferred to the church we now see. Early 20th-century Ovington was a self-contained community with a working mill, a forge and a village bakery. Today the main centre of what might be called workaday activity is its riverside pub, the Bush Inn. Tradition has it that this was a stopping place for pilgrims en route to Canterbury, although how they can ever have found it seems today a matter of mystery, so well secluded is it that few modern travellers can claim to have discovered it purely by chance. Yet people come here from all over Hampshire and well beyond, attracted by its reputation as a place apart, like the little village on the edge of which it lies.

The 'olde-worlde' style in which the landlord takes pride is reflected in the maintenance of traditional opening hours: 11 am to 2.30 pm and 6 pm to 11 pm (12 noon to 3 pm and 7 pm to 10.30 pm on Sundays). High-back seats, a central bar, three real fires in winter and a waterside garden where you can sit out in warmer weather are distinctive features, and the pub's dark interior provides an ideal setting for cosy tête-à-tête meals and meetings. Brews on tap include Flowers Original, Horndean HSB, Whitbread Strong Country and guest ales which are changed fortnightly. Murphy's Irish stout and selected lagers including Stella are available on draught as well as Bulmer's traditional cider, and there is a good range of popular keg beers. Good home-made food is a hallmark here. Game in season, including pheasant, partridge and venison, and local river trout are Bush Inn specialities. Pan-fried sirloin steak, crispy duck breast and supreme of chicken with asparagus cooked in cream, honey and whisky sauce are among other mouthwatering menu items, along with a good range of starters, vegetarian dishes and sweets. Soups, sandwiches and ploughman's with home-made bread are very popular with walkers. The same extensive menu is available whether you choose to eat in the bar or the restaurant area. Food ordering time is from 12 noon to 2 pm and 6.30 pm (7 pm on Sundays) to 9.30 pm. An extensive à la carte menu is available in the restaurant between 7.30 pm and 9.30 pm every evening except Sundays.

Telephone: 01962 732764.

- **HOW TO GET THERE:** Ovington lies at a junction of lanes nearly a mile west of the roundabout at the western end of the Alresford bypass, the A31 Winchester–Alton road, the Bush Inn being on

the right-hand side of a short cul-de-sac where the road into Ovington village bends left as you approach from this direction.

There are no buses to Ovington, but Itchen Stoke, on the route of the walk, in served by the Stagecoach Hampshire Bus Company.

- **PARKING:** The Bush Inn's rear car park is available to walkers who use the pub, and there is some parking space on the approach road from the east.
- **LENGTH OF THE WALK:** 1½ miles. Map: OS Pathfinder 1243 Winchester (North) and New Alresford (GR 562318).

THE WALK

With the Bush Inn behind you on your left, follow the road east for a few yards before turning left to follow a path through bushes and across the Itchen by a footbridge. River views here

23

almost always include a greater or lesser number of water-birds: swans, wild ducks, coots, moorhens and possibly others. Pause to take stock of them before continuing left-handed as the path turns in that direction, now with the main river to your left and a minor side-channel to your right. The waterside section of this walk and the lane from the river to Itchen Stoke follow part of the Itchen Way.

A steadily widening swathe of trees develops between you and the main river as you head west, but the right-hand channel remains alongside you all the way to where your path bridges it close to its confluence with the main channel. This is as far as many walk before turning back to the Bush Inn, thus missing completely the delights of the rest of the route, which now follows a northerly lane flanked by trees and by Itchen Stoke's cottages. On the corner on your right where you soon reach and turn right alongside the King's Worthy–Alresford road is a thatched dwelling built of exceptionally large flints – this was the village schoolhouse, but today local children go farther afield for their schooling.

Just across the road, on your left, is the parish church of St Mary, an elevated, spireless structure based in design on a Paris chapel. It was built in 1866 at the expense of the then vicar and closed just over a century later, now being looked after by the Fund for Redundant Churches, though occasional services are still held.

Continue east along a paved roadside path, at one point along which is a seat from which you can enjoy a southerly view across the lush, tree-bordered pastures of this peaceful stretch of the Itchen Valley. Where the metalled path ends turn right to follow a narrow downhill lane between trees to a watersplash flanked by a footbridge. A leftward twist of the lane passes Ovington Mill and bridges its millrace before crossing the main river.

You now turn right at a T-junction of narrow lanes to head back west with the broad sweep of the Itchen's mainstream to your right and a minor channel to your left at the foot of a steep, timbered bank. The Bush Inn now lies just ahead, on your right.

WALK 5

ALRESFORD AND THE RIVER ALRE

A duck-thronged pond, a lovely old watermill, the river Alre (pron. Ah-rl), and a path which ranks among the county's best for waterside interest and charm are yours to see and enjoy on this walk from the 'watercress capital' of Hampshire. Bring some food for the ducks.

Alresford's picturesque fulling mill

The little town of New Alresford was planned and developed 800 years ago as a centre for rural commerce. Broad Street, at its centre, dates from that period and was made deliberately wide to accommodate sheep fairs and other trade gatherings. At around the same time a high embankment was constructed across the oddly-named river Alre, one of several chalk streams that come together in this area of mid-Hampshire to create the river Itchen, and a very large lake was formed, a shrunken remnant of which survives as Old Alresford Pond. The man behind all this was a Winchester bishop, Godfrey de Lucy, who had a palace at nearby

25

Bishop's Sutton, the supply of fresh fish for which, it is nowadays thought, was the prime purpose of the great pond. New Alresford's otherwise tranquil history has been punctuated by some disastrous fires. One of the worst, in 1689, severely damaged the church. This fire and a later one in 1736 destroyed so many buildings that nearly all the attractive, mellow dwellings which characterise so much of the town today were built after that time. The 19th century brought the railway, once important for conveying local produce, including watercress, to distant markets – hence the name, the Watercress Line, by which the preserved railway between Alresford and Alton is popularly known.

The Globe on the Lake lies in an area called The Soke at the south-western end of Old Alresford Pond. Open from 11 am to 3 pm and 6 pm to 11 pm (12 noon to 3 pm and 7 pm to 10.30 pm on Sundays), it serves 'the best kept beer in Alresford', one of its regulars assured me. Marston's Pedigree and Wadworth 6X are among four real ales always available as well as draught Guinness and selected lagers. The wide range of freshly prepared bar meals includes specialities such as fish, game, vegetarian dishes and selected items for those with particular allergies. Food ordering times are 12 noon to 2 pm and 6.30 pm to 9.30 pm (12 noon to 2 pm and 7 pm to 9 pm on Sundays). Full restaurant service is available in the evenings from Tuesday to Saturday and at Sunday lunchtime, for which advance table booking is strongly advised. Telephone: 01962 732294.

- **HOW TO GET THERE:** New Alresford is now bypassed by the A31, the Winchester–Alton road, with turning-off points to it at roundabouts for those approaching from either direction. The town also has direct road links with Basingstoke and with the A272 at Cheriton via the B3046. From the main street, the B3047, the Globe will be found just round the right-hand corner at the lower end of Broad Street. Stagecoach Hampshire buses and Oakley Coaches both operate in the area.
- **PARKING:** The Globe has no car park but parking space can sometimes be found in Broad Street. The pay-and-display car park off Station Road, by Alresford station, is normally the best option.
- **LENGTH OF THE WALK:** 3 miles. Map: OS Pathfinder 1243 Winchester (North) and New Alresford (GR 588325).

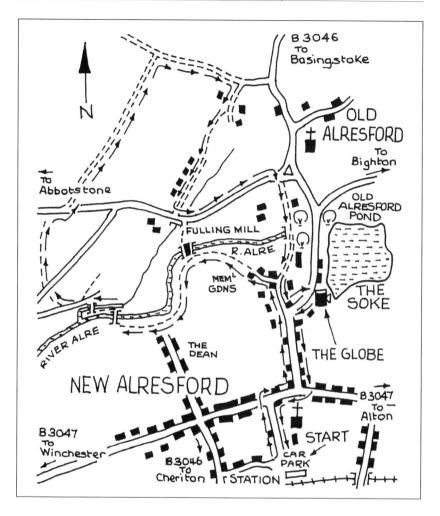

THE WALK

From New Alresford's Station Road car park follow Station Road north to join the town's main street opposite the Bell Hotel. Turn right for a few yards, then go left down well-named Broad Street, turning right at the end to follow a downhill road to the Globe on the Lake at The Soke. Public access to the water is via a pedestrian approach beside cottages to the right of the pub.

Return uphill to the bottom of Broad Street and there turn right to follow Mill Lane downhill between old buildings. Soon you turn left along Ladywell Lane, a cul-de-sac with flanking

27

cottages and paths leading to a hard-surfaced footpath with the river Alre to your right. To your left are the Alresford Memorial Gardens, on land presented to the community by the late Sir Francis Lindley to commemorate the dead of two world wars.

The river is straddled by Alresford's picturesque old fulling mill. It bears on its end wall an ancient notice more than hinting at dire penalties for any who fish here without first obtaining permission from the owner of the fishery.

Your path continues beside the river, on past the end of a road called The Dean and into increasingly rural surroundings, with trees overhanging the water and open country on either hand. Soon you bridge the Alre's swirling current as you skirt an old and derelict riverside building. With flowing water now on both sides, continue to another footbridge over the water to your right, after crossing which your path emerges through trees to join a lane, which you follow ahead.

Disregard a stile on your right between the lane and a Christmas tree plantation and continue to where a signposted footpath with steps at its base climbs right-handed. This leads to another lane, which you cross to bear left to a field gate by another footpath sign. Beyond this gate your path follows the right-hand edge of a field, over a slight hump with fine valley views before and behind you, then dropping down to a further quiet country lane.

Follow this lane right-handed for a few yards, then turn left along a signposted right of way which proves to be a very delightful hedged green lane. Within ½ mile this joins at right-angles another hedged green lane, which you follow right-handed, mainly downhill, to where a metalled farm road leads you right-handed. Disregard side-turnings and carry on ahead past houses to where a footpath sign points right-handed to a stile, beyond which you follow the left-hand edge of farmland with views towards Old Alresford church to your left.

Your path soon skirts left of some cottages to emerge onto a lane which you follow left-handed, bridging a tributary of the Alre before continuing to a point within yards of the Basingstoke–Alresford road. Turn right here to follow a metalled footpath past watercress beds, soon rising past Alresford's Town Mill and its multi-tiered cascade to join Mill Lane, which you go up to return via Broad Street, Alresford's main street and Station Road to the car park.

ROMSEY: ALONG THE OLD CANAL

This follows an old canal path along the valley of a river world-famous for its fishing. The full walk starts from Romsey and a shorter alternative route from the Duke's Head pub at Greatbridge is also described.

The Duke's Head at Greatbridge, near Romsey

The closing decades of the 18th century saw a frenzy of canal construction in many parts of England. One of the fruits of this in Hampshire was the Andover and Redbridge Canal. Some 22 miles long, with 24 locks and a rise of 169 ft from south to north, this followed a parallel course with the river Test a little way east of the river itself as far north as Fullerton, where it switched to the west side of the valley through which flows the river Anton. Not much is left. The Andover–Redbridge railway killed it and was built in part over where it once ran. The main surviving remnant is a 2-mile stretch directly north of Romsey, alongside which the former towing-path offers a pleasant waterside walk from a Test

29

Valley town which was ancient long before canals or railways became a feature of its neighbourhood.

A useful pub for refreshment en route is the Duke's Head at Greatbridge, or this can be the starting point of a shorter circuit (see map) if you wish. It was built around 1700 and originally known as the Three Tuns. The real ales here include Flowers Original, Wethered Bitter, Castle Eden and Marston's Pedigree. You will find a tempting choice of bar snacks ranging from pizza-style open baguettes, club sandwiches and ploughman's to jacket potatoes, filled canapés and a selection of hot entrées, and on Sundays many call here for a traditional three-course lunch. There is also an extensive à la carte menu in the supper room. Food ordering times are 12 noon to 2 pm and 7 pm to 9.30 pm. Children are welcome in the two end bar areas. The opening times are from 11.30 am to 2.30 pm and 5.30 pm to 11 pm on Mondays to Fridays, 11.30 am to 3 pm and 6 pm to 11 pm on Saturdays and 12 noon to 3 pm and 7 pm to 10.30 pm on Sundays. A cheering log fire in winter not only enhances the comfort but contributes to the old-world atmosphere of this delightful pub near the river Test. Telephone: 01794 514450.

- **HOW TO GET THERE:** The full-length walk begins at Romsey, reached via the A3057 from either Southampton or Andover, the A3090 and A31 from Winchester, the A31 from the New Forest, the A27 from Salisbury and the M27/A3057 from the Portsmouth and Fareham direction.

  Solent Blue Line, Southampton Citybus, Stagecoach Hampshire buses and Wilts & Dorset Bus Company all serve the area.

  If you want to start at the Duke's Head, this is approached along the A3057 Romsey–Andover road and will be found opposite the turn off to Tidworth, the B3084.

- **PARKING:** Car parks in Romsey are 'pay-and-display', the main one being off Broadwater Road, reached from Romsey bypass via Palmerston Road. Another, Orchard Lane car park, lies off Lortemore Place, reached from Romsey Market Place via The Hundred, Latimer Street and Station Road, while a third is alongside the station approach. Walkers starting from the Duke's Head and using the pub may leave their cars in the pub car park.

- **LENGTH OF THE WALK:** 4 ½ or 1 ¾ miles. Map: OS Pathfinder 1263 Romsey and Whiteparish (GR 355210 or 351232).

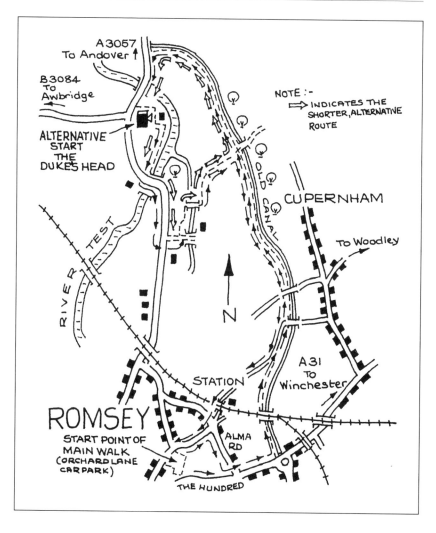

THE WALK

From Romsey town centre follow The Hundred – or from Station Road follow Alma Road – to the roundabout by the old cinema (now a theatre) at the junction of Southampton Street with Winchester Road, and there turn left to follow the old canal towing-path, with the canal itself on your right. At first the path has a metalled surface, and within a very short distance a culvert takes it under the railway, a little way beyond which another metalled path joins your own from the left.

31

Footbridges span the canal at intervals, giving access between the canalside path and the dwellings of Cupernham and Woodley. A more substantial road-bridge marks the beginning of open country, with pastures spreading to your left and, soon, on your right, alongside the canal on its far bank, a stretch of woodland in which deer can sometimes be glimpsed.

At a point where another path crosses your own, continue ahead with the gently-flowing waterway still to your right, its level – higher than some of the adjoining land – making plain its artificial origin. A small expanse of surface water on your right, just beyond the canal, comes into view almost at the same time as the Romsey–Andover road, onto which you emerge where it bridges the waterway. Follow this left-handed, crossing from one side to the other to take advantage of grass verges until you cross the Test itself and a roadside path becomes available, soon reaching the Duke's Head, on your left.

After a break here (or if this is your starting point), take the signposted footpath along a driveway directly opposite the B3084, just north of the pub. Immediately before a house at the end of the drive your path diverts a few yards to the right to reach the bank of the river Test, a wider and more full-bodied waterway than the old Andover Canal. You stay beside this until, within a few hundred yards, you rejoin the main road, which you follow left, crossing Great Bridge over the main arm of the river.

Within a further few hundred yards, turn left to follow another driveway signposted as a public footpath. Directly beyond where this bridges a branch of the Test, cross a stile on your left to follow another riverside path. Soon this path bends right, away from the river, and develops into a farm track as it heads north-east between level pastures to the path-crossing previously mentioned on the bank of the old canal.

For the shorter walk, turn left here and follow the directions already given from this point to return to the Duke's Head.

To return to Romsey, turn right where the paths cross and follow the towing-path back to the town. Where the metalled paths divide just short of the railway, this time turn right along Canal Walk to pass under the railway near the station and follow Station Road and Latimer Street back to Romsey town centre.

WALK 7
WHERWELL AND THE TEST WAY
❧❧❧

Leading from one lovely old village to another via one of the most delightful stretches of the Test Way, then back again over an attractive common, this short ramble twice crosses the river Test at scenic spots where you will want to linger awhile, if only to feed the ducks.

The White Lion, Wherwell

Mention Wherwell to anyone who knows his or her way around Hampshire and that person will instantly recall what may fairly be described as the county's most picturesque old-world village. Thatched and timber-framed dwellings of quite exceptional delight go with a setting alongside the river universally acknowledged as being the queen of English trout streams – indeed, perhaps the most famous trout-fishing water anywhere.

The White Lion Inn, where you start, claims a place of its own in local history as having once been a coaching inn. Today it is owned by Greenalls of Warrington, a name perhaps less well known here in the South than it ought to be. A more welcoming pub you will not find, and the hospitality offered more than matches the friendly atmosphere. Brews include Flowers Original, Boddingtons and Whitbread beers, Heineken and Stella lagers and draught Guinness, with Strongbow cider also on tap. A pub first and foremost and not a restaurant, the White Lion nonetheless offers varied lunchtime and supper menus ranging from sandwiches, ploughman's, baked potatoes and salads to chilli con carne, lasagne, fish dishes and steaks. An especially tasty speciality is a dish of local mushrooms topped with tomatoes, herbs and onions glazed with cheese and served with French bread. Food is served from 12 noon to 2 pm and 7 pm to 9.30 pm except on Sunday evenings. The comfortable lounge bar is complemented by a public bar with games facilities and overnight accommodation is available. Weekday opening hours are 10 am to 2.30 pm (3 pm on Saturdays) and 6 pm to 11 pm on Wednesdays to Saturdays (7 pm on Mondays and Tuesdays), while the Sunday times are 12 noon to 3 pm and 7 pm to 10.30 pm. Telephone: 01264 860317.

- **HOW TO GET THERE:** Wherwell lies at the junction of the B3420, the old, direct Winchester–Andover road, and the B3048, from Hurstbourne Priors, which crosses the A303 just south of Longparish.

  Stagecoach Hampshire buses pass through Wherwell.
- **PARKING:** Walkers who use the White Lion Inn and who first obtain permission may leave their cars in the pub's large rear car park. Roadside parking space in the village of Wherwell is limited, as is also the case at Chilbolton, an alternative starting point for this walk.
- **LENGTH OF THE WALK:** 2 miles. Maps: OS Pathfinder 1222 Andover and 1242 The Wallops (GR 389409).

THE WALK

Leaving the White Lion Inn behind you on your left, head uphill along the Andover road, across a one-time railway bridge, just left of which it is now no longer obvious where Wherwell station used to be. Passenger trains last puffed through here in 1931 on their way between Fullerton and Hurstbourne, neither of which now has a station, and it is hard to guess how a railway between the two can ever have seemed worth while.

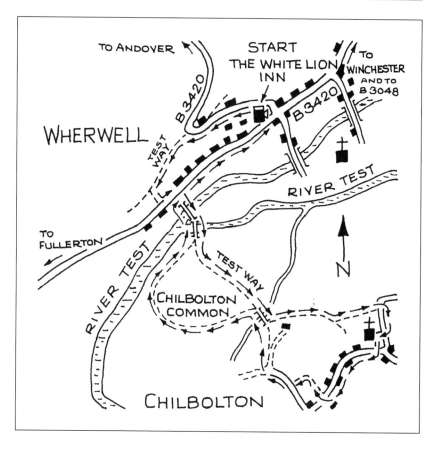

The road climbs to a sharp right-hand bend from which the Test Way strikes left through bushes before following the lower, left-hand edge of a sloping field where a chalky subsoil shows through in places. This long distance route for walkers extends from Totton, at the river Test's mouth, to Inkpen Beacon in Berkshire. Cottages now lie below you to your left as you continue to where a stepped path turns left and heads downhill to join the Fullerton–Wherwell road, which you follow left-handed when you reach it.

Within a few yards turn right along what at first is a metalled footpath to a bridge across converging channels of the tree-fringed river Test. In any case, pause for a moment or two to probe with your gaze the swirling current for possible trout.

The macadamised path continues to another, shorter,

footbridge over a lesser arm of the river. Beyond this you reach Chilbolton Common, a grassy expanse, with scattered bushes, from which cattle sometimes wallow belly-deep in the fringing waterways, a pastoral scene with overtones of pictures by Constable or Turner. Unfenced and now unmetalled, your well-used footway goes over the common to a further river footbridge. Immediately after crossing this, follow a left-turning riverside path for a matter of yards to a kissing-gate preceding another unfenced but well-defined field path. Where this divides keep left and head for a stile, beyond which you follow a road right-handed for a few yards to Chilbolton churchyard.

Local flint and chalk and some Isle of Wight stone went into the construction some 700 years ago of the small village church of St Mary-the-Less, a saint whose identity is a mystery. Whoever she may have been, the dedication to her was first celebrated during the month of August. Farmers found this inconvenient at the height of the harvest season, so William of Wykeham, the then Bishop of Winchester, changed it to a date in October.

Another path leads through the churchyard to where two roads converge towards the eastern end of Chilbolton, a Test Valley village little less well endowed with old-world charm than its neighbour Wherwell. In common with many of the lovely old cottages interspersed among others rather less ancient alongside the road you now follow right-handed, the village shop is roofed with thatch.

Opposite a left-hand cottage with a tiled roof in the middle and thatch at both ends, beyond the Abbot's Mitre pub, a hedged public footpath leads you right-handed between gardens, soon bending left to join a cul-de-sac called Joys Lane. More old dwellings flank this as it leads you right-handed back to Chilbolton Common. Here the lane becomes a track which soon divides and you bear right towards some cottages. Within yards bear left across the common along a path which soon divides in its turn after crossing the first river footbridge. Bear left here to skirt the bushy left-hand edge of the common, circling clockwise to follow the main river back to rejoin the Test Way path, which leads you left-handed back across the river to Wherwell. Reaching the road here, follow this right to the White Lion and back to your car.

BARTON STACEY: BY THE RIVER DEVER

Sample the charms of two separate rivers from the lanes and paths which pass near them at various points along this route. Quiet chalk country makes its own contribution to your enjoyment of a corner of Hampshire far from urban hustle and bustle.

The River Dever near Barton Stacey

The river Dever was not named as such on most maps until fairly recently. Normally it was given no name at all, which is why you may never have heard of it. Sometimes it was belittlingly referred to as the Bullington Stream, but any doubts that may still linger about the right of this tributary of the Test to be called a river will be set at rest when you see it in full flow as you follow this walk.

Your starting point, Barton Stacey, is a chalkland village lying in the midst of the corn-growing country north-west of Winchester. Once a royal manor, nearly all of its cottages were thatched until a devastating fire swept through in 1792. All Saints church was luckily spared, retaining to this day a mixture of Norman and Early English workmanship which can be inspected from within if you borrow a key from the village sub-post office and shop, just across the road. World War II and its aftermath brought an Army camp to the neighbourhood with married quarters for families. The military have moved on and these are now private homes like any others, standing slightly apart from the village proper, which is still steeped in an air of timeless rurality.

At its heart you will find the Swan, an honest-to-goodness country pub where traditional ales, good food and good company can be counted on. Normally open from 12 noon to 3 pm and 6 pm to 11 pm (12 noon to 3.30 pm and 7 pm to 10.30 pm on Sundays), this freehouse serves Strong Country, Flowers Original, Speckled Hen and Brains Dark Mild ale as well as Whitbread Best Bitter, Boddingtons, Heineken lagers, Murphy's Irish stout and Strongbow cider. Long-time favourites such as steak and kidney pie, chicken pie, lasagne and scampi are among the dishes to be found either as daily specials or bar menu regulars. There is a full à la carte restaurant menu and the three-course traditional Sunday lunches are very popular. Food may be ordered from 12 noon to 2.30 pm and 6.30 pm to 10.30 pm but not on Sunday evenings. Beams, exposed brickwork and an open log fire in winter help provide character and comfort.

Telephone: 01962 760470.

- **HOW TO GET THERE:** Barton Stacey lies 1 mile south of the A303 dual carriageway between Andover and the Bullington Cross A34/ A303 flyover and interchange.
  Stagecoach Hampshire buses pass through Barton Stacey.
- **PARKING:** The small village car park next to the church is often full, but walkers using the Swan may leave their cars in the pub's rear car park. Limited space for roadside parking is also available.
- **LENGTH OF THE WALK:** 4½ miles. Map: OS Pathfinder 1223 Whitchurch (Hants) (GR 435410).

THE WALK

Leaving the Swan behind you on your right, follow the main village road north through Barton Stacey and then turn left immediately past the churchyard to follow a downhill track to a kissing-gate. From this a footpath leads you diagonally right across

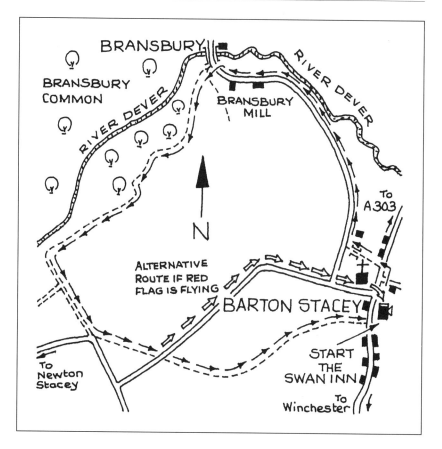

a paddock to a second kissing-gate. The path then crosses a second paddock preceding a footbridge over a stream, beyond which you emerge onto a narrow, little-used lane, which you follow right-handed.

On your right, a few yards along this lane, is an ancient chalk-rubble wall topped with traditional thatch coping, an uncommon sight these days. After a brief ascent the lane heads steadily downhill, with water in view in the Dever Valley to your right. Soon you find yourself walking parallel with the rippling river Dever, partly screened form your view at first by trees. As you head west the river draws closer, with a millrace alongside you and then the mill, now a private residence.

River and lane stay close together as far as a bridge over which the byway turns right for the hamlet of Bransbury, just ahead. Do not cross the bridge but turn left to follow a hedged track which becomes a meandering green lane, flanked by farmland on your left and by a long stretch of scrub woodland on your right.

Where the woodland ends you emerge onto Bransbury Common, a broad and bushy riverside pasture with Harewood Forest in view beyond it. The path becomes ill-defined in places but you keep as close to the common's leftward edge as conditions permit and will fairly soon see the river Test sweeping into view, not far from the point where it is joined by the river Dever. Here the fence on your left-hand side bends left and you also turn in that direction.

Pass through a gate to follow a tree-bordered track which was once a Roman road and is now a mere public path. A little way along disregard a track which turns right and keep straight on to where the track you are following joins a metalled road. Here a footpath sign points your way diagonally left across arable farmland, cutting a corner to rejoin the Chilbolton–Barton Stacey road within a few hundred yards. Cross this road by further footpath signs to continue in line with the path just followed, climbing gently to cross a low ridge of arable chalkland which is sometimes barred to public access when a red flag warns that Chilbolton firing range is in use – in which case stay on the road and follow it left-handed back to Barton Stacey. Otherwise, follow the footpath to where it joins a farm track flanked by a hedgerow. Walk along this track left-handed over undulating farmland to where it joins another farm track and you continue ahead along a field-edge path. After bridging a stream you follow the right-hand edge of a playing-field to rejoin the main village road in Barton Stacey, which you follow left-handed back to your starting point.

THE TEST AT WHITCHURCH AND LAVERSTOKE

❦

Enjoy the upper reaches of the famous River Test and the scenic valley through which it winds at their incomparable best on this walk from an old north Hampshire town which preserves a celebrated silk mill. Wooded slopes, parkland timber and wide green fields enfold the river, while overlooking the valley from both sides is rolling chalkland. If you plan to visit the mill, remember not to come on a Monday.

The White Hart Hotel in Whitchurch

The small town of Whitchurch is very ancient and originally grew around the crossing-point of two major highways – between Oxford and Southampton and between Basingstoke and Salisbury. The pre-Norman 'white church' from which it takes its name was probably built of chalk or limestone. The present parish church of All Hallows, with its dominating spire, retains a number of Norman features but was largely rebuilt in the 19th

41

century. With its nucleus of small shops serving the needs of the local community, Whitchurch preserves the atmosphere of an old-fashioned country town. Continuity with the past finds expression in many aspects of local life, in particular the survival of a silk mill now in the care of English Heritage, where robes and gowns for legal luminaries and others have long been made. Some use is still made of water-power from the Test, which provides a pleasant riverside setting, and Whitchurch Silk Mill is open to visitors every day except Mondays, from 10.30 am until 5 pm.

Where the two ancient highways intersect at the centre of Whitchurch is the White Hart Hotel, an old coaching inn which traces its history back at least to the 15th century. There is a comfortable bar where walkers often drop in for refreshment. Hours are 11 am to 11 pm (12 noon to 10.30 pm on Sundays) and brews include Courage Best, Directors and Wadworth 6X as well as Kronenbourg, Foster's and Holsten lagers, draught Guinness and Blackthorn cider. Tea and coffee are served from 9 am and food from 12 noon to 2.30 pm and 7 pm to 10 pm seven days a week. Bar snacks come in a wide variety and include cold and hot filled baguettes, pizzas, vegetarian dishes and a particularly good selection from the salad bar. For a full-blown meal there is the stylish Lord Denning Restaurant, named after a former Master of the Rolls who became a distinguished resident. Telephone: 01256 892900.

- **HOW TO GET THERE:** Whitchurch lies just east of the A34 midway between Winchester and Newbury (sliproads to it are signposted) and is reached from Andover and Basingstoke via the B3400.

    Stagecoach Hampshire buses serve the area, and trains between Basingstoke and Andover call at Whitchurch at 2-hourly intervals throughout most of the day on weekdays and Sundays.

- **PARKING:** There are free public car parks on the west side of the Winchester road next to Whitchurch Silk Mill and in Longs Court, off Church Street in Whitchurch. Roadside parking is also available, but the car park at the White Hart is of limited size and reserved for customers and residents.

- **LENGTH OF THE WALK:** 5 miles. Map: OS Pathfinder 1223 Whitchurch (Hants) (GR 463479).

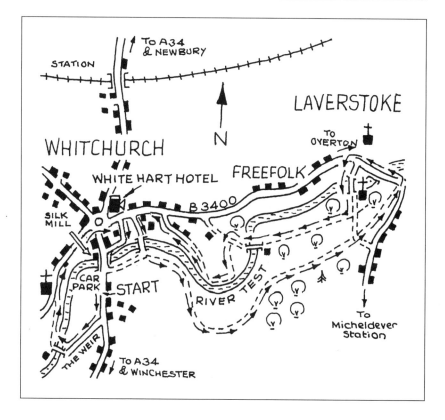

THE WALK

From the car park by the silk mill follow Winchester Road south, away from Whitchurch town centre. Not many yards after passing the Harvest Home pub on your right, turn right to follow a narrow country lane called The Weir. Cottages on your left precede fields and trees as you approach a former mill on the river Test, where you turn right to follow a hard-surfaced path with the river on your right.

Within a few hundred yards the path turns left, away from the river, with a wall topped at first with barbed-wire screening a garden on your right – the long-time home of Lord Denning backs onto this. The path joins the Andover road directly opposite Whitchurch parish church, well worth a visit before you follow Church Street east, past the King's Arms pub and Longs Court car park, to the town centre. Here five roads meet, with the White Hart Hotel in view on a corner left ahead.

43

The River Test between The Weir and the Church of All Hallows at Whitchurch

Follow London Street to (or past) the White Hart and then on past the Red House pub to take the second right-hand turning, Town Mill Lane, which is flanked by a waterway. Town Mill is the home of Ron Eastman, whose films of kingfishers and other wildlife attracted critical acclaim when televised some years ago.

By Town Mill House cross the Test itself and turn left to follow an unmetalled path, with trees and the river to your left and arable chalkland to your right. About ½ mile along this well-used public footpath, cross a stile on your left to follow a tributary path, through bushes and then along a winding valley with a timbered slope on your right. Cross a further stile, where a waymarking arrow directs you right-handed to the field edge on that side, where you turn left to follow the right-hand side of the field, with woodland rising to your right. The upper Test Valley spreads its scenic treasures to your left as you continue along the woodland edge to a gate through which you emerge onto a fenced track. Cross this and a stile just opposite to follow a downhill path across parkland, bearing slightly left-handed to skirt right of two successive large cedars.

On your right is Laverstoke village. The cottages you can see were mostly built to accommodate workers at the paper mill owned by the Portals. This French Huguenot family brought their skills to Britain 300 years ago to escape the persecution then being meted out to Protestants in Louis XIV's France. Now based in larger premises at nearby Overton, the enterprise they founded at Laverstoke has specialised in the making of paper for banknotes, British and foreign. In early days, water-power from the river Test was utilised for this purpose.

Near the bottom left-hand corner of the park you reach the Whitchurch–Basingstoke road, which you cross and follow left-handed before turning right, uphill, for a close quarters look at Laverstoke's 19th-century spired church of St Mary the Virgin. This replaced an older church in Laverstoke Park, seat of the Portals. At Freefolk, only a few yards farther west in the Whitchurch direction, a terrace of highly photogenic thatched cottages lies back behind gardens on your right. Almost opposite is a lane which leads you left-handed, bridging the Test before passing Freefolk's 13th-century church of St Nicholas. The key to this tiny, white-walled structure, now cared for by the Fund for Redundant Churches, can be obtained from a nearby cottage.

The lane leads to a track from which you turn right alongside a cottage on your right to follow a path across a long meadow, with the river downhill to your right. A line of trees straight ahead marks the route of the path, which then continues in a fairly straight line to a stile at the left-hand end of a fence at the far end of the long meadow. Continue across the next field to a stile just left of a dwelling on the far side. Here you join and follow ahead a lane which bridges the Test within view of a mill not far to your left.

A few hundred yards after crossing the river turn left from the lane to follow a well-defined footpath which converges with the Test then enters an arable field and follows its left-hand edge. The hedge on your left precedes a gap through which your path passes before developing into a track which fairly soon leads on into a road serving a modern housing development. This brings you out onto the Basingstoke road which you follow left-handed into Whitchurch. Turn left to follow Test Road over the river and then go right to reach Winchester Road almost opposite Whitchurch Silk Mill and the car park alongside it.

THE DEVER VALLEY NEAR MICHELDEVER

✦✦✦

A lovely old village and a crystal-clear chalk stream in the rural heart of Hampshire make a happy combination on this footpath-and-bridleway walk. A parish church of rather unusual design is on the route and well worth a visit.

The Dever Arms at Micheldever

At Micheldever as elsewhere, there has been a historical reluctance to recognise what is now generally known as the Dever as a river, or even to agree on its having a name of any sort. Delving into written records, we find vague references here to a North Brook, which also happens to be the name of that part of Micheldever which lies north of the brook in question. People here nowadays have no qualms at all about calling this brook the Dever and acknowledging it as a river, albeit a smallish one at this point, only a mile or so from its source. Pronounce it to rhyme with 'beaver', notwithstanding the fact that the village itself should correctly be pronounced as 'Mitchel-devver' – such, so often, are the unexplained incongruities of spoken English. The name is supposed to mean 'much water', though some dispute this, and apparently there would not be nearly so much, in any case, had the water level not been boosted by artesian bores supplying former watercress beds on the village outskirts. Micheldever is noted for its many picturesque thatched and timber-framed dwellings and for the highly unusual nave of the parish church of St Mary the Virgin, which is octagonal in shape and dates from the early 19th century. The church tower is partly constructed of stone which is thought to have been brought here from Hyde Abbey in Winchester when this was demolished after the Dissolution.

Once known as the Half Moon and Spread Eagle, the village pub is now less mysteriously named the Dever Arms. Open from 11.30 am to 3 pm and 6 pm to 11 pm on weekdays and from 12 noon to 2 pm and 7 pm to 10.30 pm on Sundays, this freehouse serves half-a-dozen selected local or regional draught ales such as Badger Best Bitter, Summer Lightning and Ringwood Best and lagers such as Carlsberg and Pilsner. Food is available from 12 noon to 2 pm and 7 pm to 10 pm (but not on Sunday evenings) and ranges from bar snacks, soup of the day and blackboard specials to full-blown à la carte restaurant meals, for which booking is advisable.

Telephone: 01962 774339.

- **HOW TO GET THERE:** If travelling northbound leave the M3 at junction 9 to follow the A33 for nearly 6 miles before turning left where a signpost points to Micheldever (1 mile). From the Basingstoke direction leave the M3 at junction 7 to follow the A30 and then the A33 for 6 miles before turning right for Micheldever. The Dever Arms is on the east side of Winchester Road, at the south-east end of Micheldever.

    Stagecoach Hampshire buses serve the area.
- **PARKING:** Customers of the Dever Arms may leave their cars in the large pub car park while walking, and there is roadside parking space in the vicinity.
- **LENGTH OF THE WALK:** 3½ miles. Map: OS Pathfinder 1243 Winchester (North) and New Alresford (GR 518389).

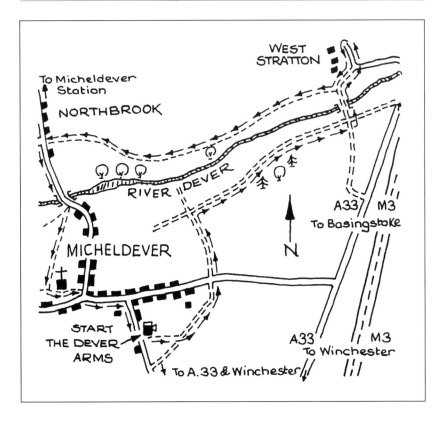

THE WALK

Begin by heading for the far right-hand corner of the cricket ground immediately behind the Dever Arms and there join a hedged track, which you follow left-handed between houses and open farmland. When you soon reach a road, cross it to follow a continuation track-cum-driveway which becomes an unfenced farm track as it leads you away from the village.

Halfway across the first bit of arable farmland is a crossing of tracks with a row of trees in view ahead of you and the westerly end of another line of tress directly parallel with the track which leads to your right here. Turn right at this point to follow what elderly local residents remember as 'the Coffin Walk' from the days before motor hearses when the dead from nearby East and West Stratton were conveyed by handcart to Micheldever for burial. The handcart in question may still be seen in Micheldever church.

After the first few hundred yards, 'the Coffin Walk', an extension of Rook Lane at Micheldever, is shaded by tall trees as you follow it east, with gently rising ground to your right and, to your left, the shallow vale which cradles the infant river Dever. After passing a small wood on your right, continue ahead to where another tree-lined track crosses your own. Turn left here and head downhill to go over the Dever by a footbridge, a little way beyond which your path becomes briefly fenced as it leads on to emerge at West Stratton, a tiny, well-thatched village on a winding, little-used lane. Savour its old-world charm before returning downhill to follow a public footpath which turns right and heads west along the right-hand side of a long field, with a hedge to your right and the Dever not very many yards to your left.

Your path draws closer to the river at one point as it leads ahead across another long field to a gateway where the hedge still to your right bends somewhat right-handed. The houses of Northbrook appear ahead here on the far side of a large field, across which you continue on a route in line with the path you have hitherto followed, with the river expanded to form miniature lakes behind trees in the valley to your left.

From the field's end your path continues between dwellings to reach the road at Northbrook opposite the turning for Weston Colley. Turn left to cross the Dever – a respectable river already, with a well-placed public seat alongside it – and take the left-hand one of two paths diverging right to reach the church, which is well worth a visit. Skirt round the church and head downhill to rejoin the road, which you follow right-handed, taking the second turning right for the Dever Arms and your walk's end.

WALK 11

DOGMERSFIELD: BY THE BASINGSTOKE CANAL

✥

Step back in time to the 18th century as you follow this peaceful canalside walk through a quiet corner of north-east Hampshire where little has changed since horses first hauled barges along this waterway. People now walk for pleasure where those horses used to labour.

The Barley Mow, on the Basingstoke Canal near Winchfield

The only inland waterway in Hampshire which is navigable today is the Basingstoke Canal, opened in 1796 as a route for the conveyance of heavy merchandise to and from London and the coast by way of the rivers Wey and Thames. Like so many other canals built around that time, this one had a very short life as a viable enterprise. Decline set in with the arrival of really serious competition in 1839, when the London–Southampton railway was opened as far as Basingstoke, and 30 years later the operating company was wound up. There was a brief later restoration and revival, but commercial traffic finally ceased in the early 20th century. Desultory leisure use continued for a time, and then for many years the waterway lay derelict and neglected. It suffered what seemed a mortal blow to any hopes of a second revival when the canal tunnel roof at Greywell, north of Odiham, collapsed. In the 1960s, however, a group of enthusiasts launched the Surrey and Hampshire Canal Society. By the early 1990s bridges had been repaired and strengthened, the towing-path made good once more and it was again possible for pleasure craft to ply the waterway. Many have thus rediscovered the charm of this part of northern Hampshire, otherwise largely inaccessible, where time appears to have stood still.

Your walk starts at the Barley Mow, an Ushers house on the outskirts of the little village of Dogmersfield, between Odiham and Fleet. Open on weekdays from 11 am to 2.30 pm and 6 pm to 11 pm and on Sundays from 12 noon to 2.30 pm and 7 pm to 10.30 pm, this pub lies in quiet countryside within yards of the canal. Traditional ales served here include – no prizes for guessing – Ushers Best, Founders and Four Seasons Ales as well as Courage Best. There is also a choice of lagers, including Hofmeister and Kronenbourg, or perhaps your taste is for Guinness or Beamish stout – all of which are on draught here. Food is available from 12 noon to 2 pm and 7.15 pm to 9.15 pm and the lunchtime menu offers a good choice of ploughman's, sandwiches and jacket potatoes alongside steaks, fish dishes, omelettes, macaroni cheese and other home-cooked specials. Vegetarians are catered for and there is a separate children's menu. As well as the main restaurant, which offers an evening à la carte menu, there is a conservatory eating area for non-smokers. A log fire in winter and a patio and garden for fine and sunny days in spring and summer are other attractions. Telephone: 01252 617490.

- **HOW TO GET THERE:** Approaching from the M3, leave at junction 5 and follow the B3349 to Hook, where you join and follow the A30 for just over 2 miles in the London direction before turning sharp right at Phoenix Green, just short of Hartley Wintney, to follow the B3016 for a mile. After going under the M3 turn left just short of a railway bridge to pass Winchfield station on your right. Disregard the first turning right from the winding lane you now follow, then at a crossroads ½ mile further on turn right to reach the Barley Mow within a few hundred yards, on your left.

Stopping trains between Basingstoke and Waterloo call at Winchfield ½-hourly on weekdays and hourly on Sundays, it being a 1½-mile walk from Winchfield station to the Barley Mow along the route outlined above.

- **PARKING:** Walkers using the Barley Mow may leave their cars in the pub car park and there is a separate free car park beside the canal, only yards away.
- **LENGTH OF THE WALK:** 3½ miles. Map: OS Pathfinder 1204 Basingstoke (GR 778538).

THE WALK

From the Barley Mow cross the public car park to join Basingstoke Canal towing-path a few yards east of Barley Mow Bridge. With the bridge behind you and the canal on your right, follow the hard-surfaced towing-path as it curves right with the canal, changing direction from east to south. Houses in Dogmersfield village can be glimpsed on your left, the road that serves them at first running closely parallel with the canal and then diverging from it, with fields and woodlands intervening.

At one stage the canal cleaves through a cutting, followed by an embankment with the water at a higher level than the bordering land. Pines and rhododendrons on the canal's far side precede a gap through which a wider expanse of water reveals itself – 20-acre Tundry Pond, a prime feature of Dogmersfield Park, which you will enter after leaving the towing-path at Blacksmith's Bridge, just around the corner from where you now stand.

Cross the bridge and then a stile to join a fenced track which angles right and then left around arable land to skirt the south side of Tundry Pond, a haven for Canada geese and wild ducks. Crowning higher ground and overlooking the park from your left is Dogmersfield House, built in 1728 on the site of a one-time bishop's palace. As the seat of the Mildmay family, at the turn of the 18th century it saw Dogmersfield village moved, lock, stock and barrel, to where it is now, so as not to impinge upon the view. A few years earlier Sir Henry Mildmay had compelled the canal company to divert their intended waterway in a wide loop

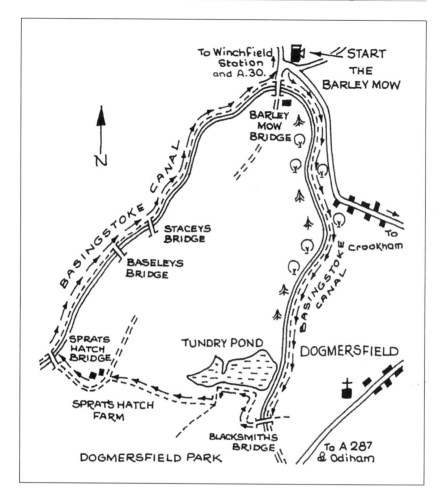

around Dogmersfield Park as another move to protect his privacy.

Centuries earlier Henry VI often stayed at Dogmersfield, and it was here that plans were made for the short-lived marriage of Henry VII's son and heir, Arthur, to Catherine of Aragon who, when widowed, became the first wife of Henry VIII. This monarch's dissolution of abbeys and other religious houses led in its turn to Dogmersfield becoming one of the many properties of his Chancellor, Thomas Wriothesley, the first Earl of Southampton.

Where Tundry Pond narrows and is spanned by a bridge, turn left towards Dogmersfield House along a fenced estate road, then after a very short distance cross a stile on your right. Two

53

The Basingstoke canal, near Dogmersfield

separate waymarked footpaths diverge here. Follow the right-hand one, heading slightly to the right of straight ahead, with the pond still on your right.

You now make your way across open ground towards Sprat's Hatch Farm and its outbuildings – as delightfully secluded a place of residence as any country-lover could wish for. When you reach the farm precincts, cross another stile and then follow a bridleway left-handed, heading by way of a green lane to Sprat's Hatch Bridge across the canal. From the far side of this you descend right-handed to join the towing-path once more. Heading north-east now, with the canal on your right, you can cast your eye towards the London–Southampton railway, a distant intrusion into a scene otherwise little altered since the very early days of the canal. Occasional isolated dwellings only serve to emphasise the peace of their immediate surroundings.

Two further brick arches span the canal before a third one, Barley Mow Bridge, signals the end of your excursion on foot through this lovely, unspoilt area.

WALK 12

FROYLE AND THE WEY VALLEY
◆◆◆

The river Wey, between Alton and the Hampshire–Surrey border, draws its substance from the enfolding chalk which also makes a big scenic contribution to this walk. Field paths and lovely lanes play their part, too. Crossing the river four times, this ramble in hop-growing country offers an outing of particular delight that deserves to be ranked among your favourites.

The Hen and Chicken, Froyle

Maps of north-east Hampshire show two rivers called the Wey. One has its source in the pine-and-heather country of the Weald, not far from Liphook, from which it meanders north-east into Surrey, where at Tilford it is joined by its namesake and twin, which rises near Alton. For the first few miles at least of this Alton version its waters have that crystalline clarity characteristic of Hampshire chalk streams, and the valley through which it winds is dominated scenically by the gentle-contoured chalk which contributes so much to our county's charm. Froyle itself shelters under the North Downs, between Holybourne and

Bentley and just to the north of the A31, and is perhaps best known as the setting for the Lord Mayor Treloar School, which caters for disabled children.

Your starting point is the Hen and Chicken Inn, which is at least 400 years old and was once a place of call for itinerant merchants as well as for the local farming community. Largely reconstructed after a fire in the 18th century, at one stage the pub became a gathering place on Sundays for rowdy elements dealing in horses and other livestock, apparently including poultry, hence perhaps the name by which the inn has been known ever since. One Sunday the local squire was so annoyed at being delayed by this unruly rabble while on his way to church at Alton that he intervened and put a stop to Sunday opening at the pub, a ban which was not lifted until 1955.

The Hen and Chicken today is deservedly popular with travellers and with local people alike, and has a distinctly upmarket image with a reputation for good food. A special dispensation in the Alton licensing area allows the pub to open on weekdays at 10 am, although 11 am is more usual, with all-day opening until 11 pm, Sunday hours (no horse-trading now!) being 12 noon to 10.30 pm. The real ales include London Pride, Flowers Original, Courage Best and a guest. Guinness and Murphy's are on draught here as well as three lagers and two ciders. Food may be ordered from 11.30 am (12 noon on Sundays) to 3 pm and 6 pm to 10 pm. Among the bar snacks are omelettes, Cumberland sausages, chicken fillets with French fries, ploughman's and a choice of sandwiches. There is a children's menu too. A separate restaurant area with waiter service offers a comprehensive à la carte menu which includes vegetarian specials, while steaks from the chargrill are much in demand, as are traditional Sunday roasts. A log fire enhances winter comfort and there is a children's outdoor play area.

Telephone: 01420 22115.

- **HOW TO GET THERE:** The Hen and Chicken lies on a service road parallel with the London-bound carriageway of the A31, 3 miles on the Farnham side of Alton. It is accessible from both carriageways of the A31.

  Stagecoach Hampshire buses pass the pub at regular intervals.

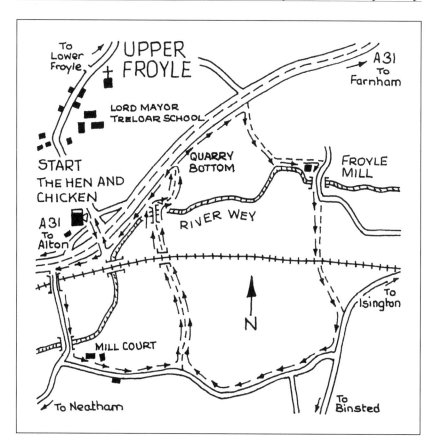

- **PARKING:** Walkers using the Hen and Chicken may leave their cars in the pub's large car park, and there is some parking space on the adjacent service road.
- **LENGTH OF THE WALK:** 4½ miles. Map: OS Pathfinder 1224 Lasham and Alton (North) (GR 756422).

THE WALK

Watch out for fast traffic as you cross from the Hen and Chicken to the south side of the A31 dual carriageway and then turn right, with the road on your right. Within 200 yards or so turn left to follow a lane over a railway bridge and then very soon across the river Wey, on which is a weir between yourself and the timber-framed former mill house forming a backdrop to the picturesque view on your right.

The River Wey at Mill Court, near Froyle

Trees shade the grounds of Mill Court, a large house approached by a drive on your left, as you continue to a lane junction with a steep, timbered bank rising beyond it. Turn left here and climb between trees and dwellings as you follow a single-track byway little used by motor traffic, soon emerging into the open with arable farmland on both sides.

Carry on to where a footpath sign points your way left-handed along a field track, where the Wey Valley spreads before you, with wood-capped downland rising beyond. Where the first field ends angle slightly left as you head downhill to a railway underbridge preceded and followed by stiles. From here your path continues ahead, with the remains of an old wall on your right, to skirt a cattle-crush and lead through a gateway to a footbridge over a quiet stretch of the Wey.

Trees shade your path, which at first leads straight on beyond the river and then climbs a steepish bank right-handed to a stile where you enter and cross a pasture. Bearing slightly left-handed of a timbered right-hand slope directly below which the river winds, you reach and cross another stile to follow right-handed the southerly verge of the A31. To your right here is Quarry Bottom, a wooded hollow where in times gone by highwaymen lurked. Earlier still, this neighbourhood was notorious for robbers who preyed on merchants travelling between Winchester and Guildford at the time of St Giles Fair.

Where trees on your right end, turn right from the road verge to cross a stile and follow a well-defined path across an arable field, with the Wey Valley dipping before you. At the field's far end your path bends left to follow a right-hand fence, along the slope and then downhill to a stile, beyond which a green track leads you left-handed. The river Wey coils below trees to your right as you carry on to where a stile on your left precedes a point where your path skirts left of farm buildings to join a lane, which you follow right-handed. You now descend to pass old Froyle Mill, now a private house, and cross the river Wey again. Your lane then climbs to a leftward bend where you cross a stile directly ahead. A signposted path leads to a second stile, then to a somewhat decrepit third one, beyond which you bear half-right to climb to the right-hand end of the hedge on the far side of the pasture you now cross.

Pause here to enjoy the Wey Valley view behind you before going over a stile to follow a path with a hop garden to your left and a wood to your right. This leads to another stile and a stepped path down a steep-sided cutting to the single-track Alton–Farnham railway, and after crossing this you climb to a further stile, beyond which the path angles slightly right across a paddock to the next stile. Here a footpath sign points your way across arable farmland, again angling slightly right as you converge with the leftward edge of the field, which you leave by another stile to follow a lane leading right-ahead.

At a lane-fork, within yards, bear right and head west for ½ mile as far as a footpath sign pointing right-handed. Follow this to sample again the first cross-country path on this walk, back across the Wey Valley to the A31. When you reach this busy road, turn left to follow its southerly verge to where the Hen and Chicken and your walk's end beckon across the dual carriageway.

THE RIVER MEON AT DROXFORD

Hampshire's Meon Valley is a byword for scenic beauty, and no part of it more so than its middle reaches, near old-world Droxford. Angling author Izaak Walton once fished for trout where you will walk here.

The cross-river path over the Meon

The river Meon, less substantial than either the Itchen or the Test, has its source in the South Downs half-a-dozen miles south-west of Petersfield and threads its quiet way to the coast through a succession of old-world villages of which Droxford is one of the largest and indisputably the most ancient. A settlement of some sort almost certainly existed in this location before the Jutish Meonwara, after whom the valley is named, were converted to the Christian faith by St Wilfrid in the 7th century. A cemetery of that period came to light here when the Meon Valley railway was being constructed.

With the railway came a new hostelry, the Railway Hotel, a matter of yards from Droxford station, at Brockbridge, on the

60

Droxford–Hambledon road. After the railway closed in 1955 this became the Meon Valley Hotel and then, in course of time, the Hurdles, a smart and popular pub-restaurant well used to catering for walkers. Traditional licensing hours of 11 am to 2.30 pm and 6 pm to 11 pm (12 noon to 2.30 pm and 7 pm to 10.30 pm on Sundays) are still observed at this freehouse, which offers a warm, friendly welcome. Real ales on tap include Marston's pedigree, Gale's HSB and Ansells Best Bitter. There are also three draught lagers as well as draught Guinness and Old English cider, while wine drinkers can choose from an especially large selection including Gale's country wines. Food may be ordered from 12 noon to 2 pm and 7 pm to 10 pm (from 6.30 pm on Saturdays) and is all home-made by the pub's own chefs. The bar menu offers a good choice of starters, fish dishes, steaks, pies and snacks including sandwiches for those who prefer something less than a full meal. Also available in the evening, from 7 pm to 10 pm, is a separate and comprehensive dining room menu, with table service (booking advisable). Special catering arrangements can be made for organised parties.
Telephone: 01489 877451.

- **HOW TO GET THERE:** The Hurdles at Brockbridge lies on the south side of the B2150, the Droxford–Waterlooville road, ¼ mile east of where this leaves the A32, the Fareham–Alton road, opposite Merington's garage at the north end of Droxford village.
  Solent Blue Line and People's Provincial buses serve the area.
- **PARKING:** Walkers who first obtain permission may leave their cars in the Hurdles' car park. There is limited space for parking in adjacent Station Road – or on the approach road to Droxford church if you start the walk there instead of at Brockbridge.
- **LENGTH OF THE WALK:** 2½ miles. Map: OS Pathfinder 1285 Horndean (GR 615185).

THE WALK

From the Hurdles walk under the railway bridge just to the west, then disregard the road that immediately turns left but take the second one, a few yards further on, a cul-de-sac which heads downhill obliquely away from the B2150 with right-hand views across typical Meon Valley pastures through which winds the river Meon itself. Rivers and other watery areas attract their own

61

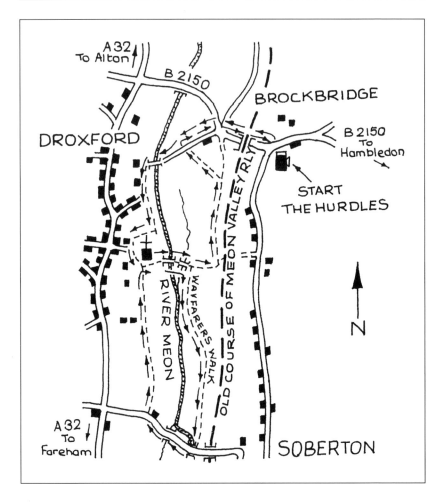

particular birdlife, sometimes including comparative rarities like the snowy-white little egret, somewhat like a miniature heron, which I have seen here.

The narrow lane ends and a macadamised footpath begins just short of a footbridge across the river where it is joined on your left by a tributary stream. With the waterway now alongside it, the footpath leads to another footbridge, over the millrace by Droxford's old mill, at the end of another cul-de-sac from which, within yards, you bear left to follow a field path along the right-hand edge of a paddock to the nearside corner of Droxford churchyard.

Here a path leads you right-handed with the churchyard on your left. The round-headed Norman doorway on the north side of the parish church of St Mary and All Saints has a counterpart on the south side, the inner nave walls and the chancel arch being equally ancient. Izaak Walton, who wrote that fisherman's classic *The Compleat Angler* and who was familiar with the quality of fishing in the Meon, worshipped here in the 17th century when visiting his daughter, Anne, who married a rector of Droxford.

Walk round the church to its south-west corner and pass through a kissing-gate there to turn left and follow a path which is tree-lined as it leads you to a footbridge over the river Meon's main channel. Pause here to enjoy the scenic blend of tree-bordered pasture and crystal-clear water before continuing to a second footbridge, over a minor Meon sidestream.

Beyond this turn right to cross a stile and follow a section of the Wayfarer's Walk, a long distance route from Emsworth to Inkpen Beacon in Berkshire. Your path veers gradually away from the river channel to your right, crossing three more stiles and passing at one point through a cluster of tall trees close to the old Meon Valley railway before reaching a further stile where you emerge onto a lane.

Follow this right-handed, parallel with a river channel, and cross the mainstream of the Meon by a cottage on your right. Here bear right to pass through a V-shaped livestock barrier and pedestrian access point to a northbound footpath along the right-hand side of a river valley pasture. Soon cross a stile and continue ahead to where the field boundary to your right bends sharply right. You now angle slightly left across a large pasture to where a clear footpath course directs you past hedged gardens on your left to another stile. Cross this and continue to where a further stile precedes a walled and fenced path which you follow ahead to where you previously left the churchyard. Here turn right to follow again the path across the two river footbridges, and then continue uphill to where a footpath sign points your way left-handed through a sloping belt of valley-side scrub. A twisty footway leads you to a path-fork where you bear left to rejoin your original lane. Follow this uphill back to Brockbridge and the Hurdles.

WALLINGTON'S RIVER ESTUARY

❧❀❧

From an old and half-forgotten village just outside Fareham, this walk traces the twists and turns of a broadening tidal estuary to where it spills into Portsmouth Harbour. As you follow the tree-fringed banks of this inlet you will be exploring one of Hampshire's more neglected scenic treasures.

Surrounded on all sides by busy highways, the little riverside village of Wallington is an oasis of timeless tranquillity often overlooked by strangers, and is all the more worth visiting on that account alone. History, like the ceaseless hustle and bustle of modern life as most of us know it, has largely passed Wallington by since it first functioned as 'a farmstead or village of the Britons', as at least one place-name pundit explains its likely origin. The river which shares the name of the village meets salt water here after a brief but serpentine course around the western shoulder of Ports Down, that isolated chalky eminence which overlooks Portsmouth from the north. Serpentine too is the Wallington estuary, the twists and turns of which are fringed on its east side by grass and trees as you follow them on the scenic outward stages of this walk.

Once known as the Fort Wallington after the stronghold of that name built on Ports Down when France under Napoleon III seemed to threaten invasion in the mid-19th century, the village pub which later became the Wallington Tavern is now called the Cob and Pen. Cobs and pens – male and female swans – can often be seen on the river bank nearby, so the name is appropriate. Open from 11 am to 11 pm (12 noon to 10.30 pm on Sundays), this Whitbread house serves food from 12 noon to 3 pm daily and from 7 pm to 9 pm on Thursdays, Fridays and Saturdays. Bar meals range from jacket potatoes with various fillings and club sandwiches to home-cooked fare such as pie of the day, lasagne, chicken curry and chilli and rice to seafood platter, plaice and ships, sweet and sour chicken and omelettes. Sunday roasts are a special favourite. Children are welcome in the restaurant and in the large garden, a popular venue for summer barbecues. Flowers Original, Marston's Pedigree and Boddingtons are normally complemented by guest ales. Draught Guinness and Murphy's, Heineken, Stella and various bottled lagers are also available in this pub where exposed brickwork and areas of flagstone flooring help emphasise the traditional character.

Telephone: 01329 221624.

- **HOW TO GET THERE:** Bracketed by the M27, the A27 and the A32, Wallington lies just beyond the eastern extremity of Fareham. To reach it leave the M27 at the turn-off for Fareham East (junction 11). At the next interchange (Wallington flyover and roundabout) leave the Fareham approach road and take the fourth exit from the roundabout to follow Wallington Shore Road into Wallington, where the Cob and Pen pub is on your right.

  Trains from and to Southampton, Eastleigh, Winchester and Portsmouth call at Fareham at least hourly on weekdays and Sundays. People's Provincial buses and Red Admiral buses both serve the area.

- **PARKING:** Walkers using the Cob and Pen may leave their cars in the pub car park but should first obtain permission, especially on

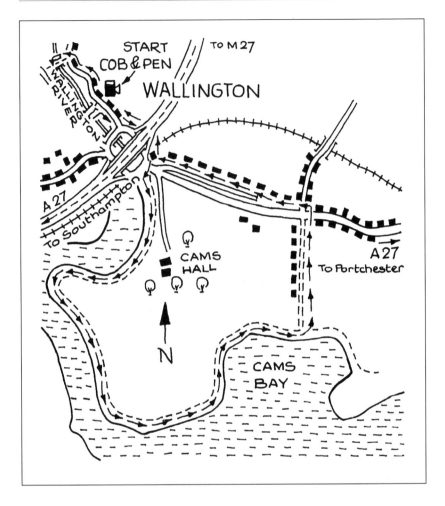

busy days such as Fridays. There is also some space for parking
alongside Wallington Shore Road.
- **LENGTH OF THE WALK:** 3½ miles. Map: OS Pathfinder 1284
Southampton Water and Fareham (GR 586065).

THE WALK

Take a preliminary peep at some of Wallington's old-world
charms by walking on beyond the Cob and Pen with period
dwellings alongside you. Many who lived in them at one time
would have worked at the local tannery, a principal source of
employment until the early 20th century.

66

Not far beyond another pub – the White Horse – a footbridge on your left will take you across the Wallington River to join a path which you follow back, parallel with the way you came, to a second footbridge. Here you regain the river's east bank and the road leading out of the village, with the river and perhaps some of its swans on your right.

Now keep to the left side of Wallington roundabout, passing the Roundabout Hotel and going under the flyover and the Fareham–Portsmouth railway. Reaching the turn-off for Portchester and Cosham by the Delmé Arms pub, cross the main road to join and follow a gravel path with the Wallington River, now tidal, to your right. Your path converges with a road serving the 'business village' now up and running around Cams Hall, which was once the home of the Delmé family.

Most of the surrounding former farmland is now a golf course, whose grassy acres spread to your left as you keep to the track closest to the estuary edge. Through trees you can look across to Fareham, where trains rumble over the Wallington viaduct at fairly frequent intervals. As the widening estuary wriggles around Cams golf course the scene becomes increasingly rural.

At Cams Bay a large flotilla of brent geese rode on the flood-tide as I passed. From here carry on past a wood on the left along a track which curves away from the water's edge beyond a gate at the end of the golf course. The track matures into a road called Birdwood Grove, which leads you back onto the A27, halfway between Portchester and Fareham. Turn left along this and cross over when convenient to join and follow left-handed Cams Hill, the parallel service road. Leading off from this is Paradise Lane, a byway whose undoubted enchantments I did not have time to sample as I headed back past the Delmé Arms to Wallington and the walk's end.

To enjoy this and other coastal walks at their best, choose a day and a time, if you can, when the tide will be high, although a compensating factor at low tide is the wealth of birdlife frequently visible, probing for food in the miry ooze receding salt water has left exposed.

WALK 15

TITCHFIELD AND THE LOWER MEON VALLEY

Tranquil Titchfield had its own canal to the coast for a brief period. Much of the waterway survives and, with it, a path leading down to the Solent shore where a clifftop walk will complete a memorably extra-special outing.

The Bugle Hotel in old-world Titchfield

If ever there was a haven of tranquillity in village form, that haven is surely Titchfield, tucked away amid rural greenery yet so very close to that urban development that almost unites Southampton and Portsmouth. Here lovely old dwellings flank ancient ways to which traffic-calming measures have restored a degree of quiet hardly matched since pre-motoring times. Fittingly, Titchfield's church of St Peter is one of the oldest in the county, with a history dating back to when St Wilfrid converted the Jutes of the Meon Valley to Christianity, or soon after. Its Saxon porch survives along with the characteristic workmanship of Norman and later periods. Less visually evident today is Titchfield's origin as a seaport at the head of a tidal estuary. It remained so until after Titchfield Abbey was dissolved by Henry VIII and the abbey lands made over by him to his Chancellor, Thomas Wriothesley, the first Earl of Southampton. In the early 17th century the third Earl had the estuary closed off at the seaward end and a canal constructed by Titchfield to allow barge traffic to continue while much of the former tidal area was transformed into watermeadows. Within quite a short time the canal fell into disuse and, its seaward exit closed, it remains in being to this day as a freshwater channel with a path alongside it where barge-horses once trod – now a great favourite with walkers.

The Bugle Hotel is one of several excellent pubs in Titchfield. A 17th-century coaching inn, the clientele today is drawn from a wide surrounding area to a pub which is open all day – from 11 am to 11 pm on weekdays and 12 noon to 10.30 pm on Sundays. Brews served here include Boddingtons, Flowers Original, Wadworth 6X and a guest ale, with Murphy's Irish stout, Strongbow and Scrumpy cider and selected lagers also on draught. Wines from many countries and 100 malt whiskies are always in stock. Food may be ordered from 12 noon to 2 pm and 7 pm to 10 pm on weekdays and all day on Sundays, when the traditional roasts are much in demand. Fresh seafood is a Bugle speciality. Daily chef's dishes complement the regular bar menu, which offers a wide choice including four different ploughman's and six continental-style open sandwiches as well as vegetarian dishes. Four-course 'winter specials' are available in season, or you can opt for the à la carte restaurant menu in the evenings and at Sunday lunchtimes. There is a family room for children and a large restaurant at the rear. Old beams, period bow windows and a flagstone floor at the entrance, not to mention an open log fire in winter, all contribute to the traditional character of this ancient hostelry at the heart of a truly old-world village. Telephone: 01329 841888.

- **HOW TO GET THERE:** Titchfield lies just off the A27 some 2 miles west of Fareham, approaches being clearly signposted. The walk starts from the little canalside car park (see parking details) which is reached from Bridge Street, the continuation of South Street, south of the main village square.

People's Provincial buses and Red Admiral buses serve the area.

- **PARKING:** There is a small free car park for canal path walkers alongside Bridge Street, where this crosses the old canal, but this often becomes full at busy times. A larger free car park off Southampton Hill can be used for a maximum stay of 3 hours, and the Bugle Hotel's own rear car park may be used by walkers who are also customers and who first obtain permission. Alternative limited free parking space may be found along West Street and some other village roads.
- **LENGTH OF THE WALK:** 5 miles. Map: OS Pathfinder 1284 Southampton Water and Fareham (inn GR 543054; Bridge Street car park GR 542054).

THE WALK

Starting from the canalside car park off Bridge Street, follow a metalled track south from the road to a second gate, from which point the Lower Meon Valley Trail, as this is now officially waymarked, becomes a meadow path (soft underfoot in winter).

The waterway lies to your right, its artificial origin emphasised by the straight course it follows, flanked on one side by your footpath and by a line of trees on the other with very few breaks for the next 2 miles. Every so often you pass through another gate or cross a stile, and there is a subsequent short section where your path becomes a metalled farm track before this gives way to gravel and then to grass and plain earth once more. Watermeadows to your left visibly live up to their name in several places and are overlooked by a timbered slope which screens from view much modern development on that side of the Meon Valley.

Continue along the canal path to emerge onto the Titchfield–Meon Shore road where this spans the canal on a sharp bend. The low bridge here is a restored version of the sea-lock through which barge traffic had to pass to enter the freshwater canal and so reach Titchfield. Opposite it is a stile beyond which you join a tree-lined path continuing south beside Titchfield Haven Nature Reserve, a county council-owned sanctuary for many species of water-birds, including a number of rarities. Boardwalks ease your way where wet ground encroaches onto the path, from which

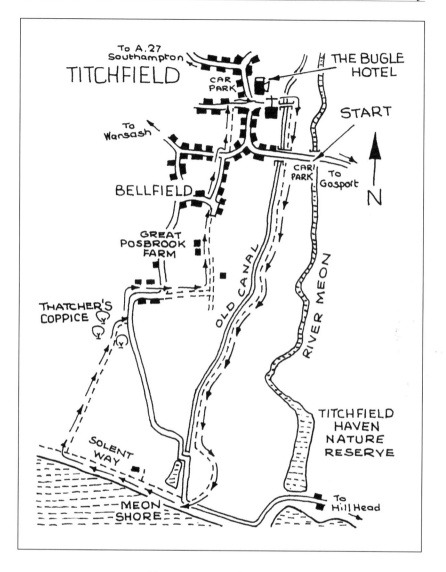

you emerge over a stile on your right to cross the road by Meon Shore, where another stile precedes a footpath with beach chalets on both sides.

Where the chalets end, turn left towards the beach to join and follow right-handed the coastal path – the Solent Way – which goes along the top of a gravelly cliff with the sea on your left. Bushes sheltering the path along much of its length are punctuated by gaps through which you can see right across the Solent to the Isle of Wight beyond. Within ½ mile turn right to cross a stile and follow a fenced path between fields to Thatcher's Coppice, where your path winds through oaks and hazels before emerging through a car park onto the Titchfield–Meon Shore road.

As you follow this left it soon bends right to another bend, where it turns left but from which a farm road which doubles as a footpath leads ahead. Follow this to a crossing of metalled farm roads, where you turn left. Beyond a semi-bungalow a short distance ahead on your right the farm road gives way to a field-edge footpath, leading straight on with a hedge to your right and the Meon Valley dipping beyond. Continue ahead to a stile, a few yards beyond which another stile precedes a fenced path with the tree-fringed grounds of Great Posbrook Farm on your left. A third stile precedes a meadow where you keep straight on to a fourth stile leading to Bellfield housing estate.

After crossing this stile bear right to reach Ransome's Close, which you follow left to join Hewett Road, turning left again to join and follow right-handed Lower Bellfield. You will then come to Coach Hill, which you follow right for a few yards, then take a macadamised footpath which turns left. This soon crosses another road and is flanked by a very old wall partly constructed of herringbone brickwork before emerging onto West Street.

Old-world Titchfield spreads before you as you continue downhill to the village square, with the Bugle Hotel almost opposite. The steepled church beckons at the end of narrow Church Street, straight ahead – spare time if you can for at least a brief visit. To the right of the chancel, in an exhibition area, is the massive Wriothesley Memorial, to the family who owned Titchfield after the abbey was closed down. A path to the right of the church leads to a footbridge across the canal, which you follow right-handed back to Bridge Street and the car park on the far side of it.

WALK 16

THE HAMBLE AT BURSLEDON

From a riverside pub made famous by the TV series 'Howard's Way', this walk explores the quieter reaches of an otherwise yacht-thronged estuary. A well-wooded country park, a farm from the past and what remains of a very old church are other attractions.

The Bursledon riverside pub featured in the TV series 'Howard's Way'

While the freshwater Hamble, above Botley, is one of Hampshire's shorter rivers, the tidal estuary into which it flows is the longest in the county. Between Bursledon and Southampton Water the Hamble estuary is also one of the busiest in Britain, with more yachts and other pleasure craft per square kilometre of water than almost any other seaway in these islands or anywhere else. The upper reaches of the estuary, between Bursledon and Botley, could hardly be more different. Except at its southernmost extremity, its banks are bereft of boatyards and all those other supporting services of the leisure sailing industry which are so much in evidence farther downstream. This tideway, until not long ago Hampshire's best-kept scenic secret,

73

revealing its charms to none except the most venturesome explorers of little-known byways, afloat or on foot, is now shared with all who visit the Hampshire County Council-owned Upper Hamble Country Park, which safeguards the superb stretch of riverside country for public enjoyment.

Where better to get the feel of this area than the Jolly Sailor pub at Bursledon, a watering hole *par excellence* for people who love salt water and lastingly famous for having featured in the TV soap opera *Howard's Way?* The pub has its own pontoon and is more accessible by boat than by any other form of transport, crouching as it does on the water's edge below a steep slope which denies it the possibility of possessing its own car park.

Once Church property and the home of a local clergyman, this was originally a cottage which had no links with the licensed trade until, 100 years ago or so, it was sold to a Southampton brewer. It later passed through several ownerships, Edwards' Brewery of Botley being proprietors at one stage. Since 1987 it has belonged to Hall & Woodhouse, whose range of Badger beers are a prime attraction at this deservedly popular pub. Open on Mondays to Fridays from 11 am to 2.30 pm and 6 pm to 11 pm and all day on Saturdays (11 am to 11 pm) and Sundays (12 noon to 10.30 pm), the Jolly Sailor serves food from 12 noon to 2 pm and 6.30 pm to 9.30 pm on Mondays to Fridays and from 12 noon to 2.30 pm and 6.30 pm to 9.30 pm on Saturdays and Sundays. Real ales include Badger Best, Tanglefoot, Hard Tackle and Jolly Sailor, a summer special, as well as Wadworth 6X. Guinness and three Hofbrau lagers are also on draught. For food you are spoilt for choice with an extensive bar menu listing main courses, 'health options' and vegetarian dishes as well as salads, ploughman's, basket meals, open and conventional sandwiches and children's favourites. There are daily blackboard specials too. The restaurant menu offers a wide choice for those who contemplate a leisurely evening meal, dining à la carte. Old beams, a flagstone floor and bull's-eye window panes looking out onto the river all help preserve an old-world atmosphere, further enhanced in recent years by the addition of an unobtrusive extension in the shape of an old barn. A log fire helps to keep the pub cosily warm in winter.

Telephone: 01703 405557.

- **HOW TO GET THERE:** Bursledon lies on the A27 halfway between Southampton and Fareham. The walk starts from the car park at Bursledon station (see parking details below).

  Southampton–Fareham trains call at roughly hourly intervals on weekdays and Sundays. The area is served by People's Provincial buses.

- **PARKING:** The free car park at Bursledon station, reached by turning right from the A27 immediately before the railway bridge if approaching from Southampton and then taking first left, is the best place to park.

- **LENGTH OF THE WALK:** 5 miles. Maps: OS Outdoor Leisure 22 New Forest and Pathfinder 1284 Southampton Water and Fareham (inn GR 492093; station car park GR 490096).

THE WALK

For some preliminary refreshment, follow a stepped and metalled footpath which climbs through trees from the right-hand side of Bursledon station car park, as you enter it. When you join a road at the top, turn left across a railway arch to pass the entrance to Elephant Boatyard, the name of which commemorates that of Nelson's flagship at the battle of Copenhagen, one of a number of men-of-war which were built on the river Hamble hereabouts in the days of sail. A few yards further on a stepped path descends to the Jolly Sailor on the river bank below.

Another path climbs back for you to return to Bursledon station, from which you follow Station Road and Church Lane to cross the A27 with care between the railway bridge and Mulligan's Fish Restaurant (formerly the Swan Hotel). Blundell Lane now leads straight on, and where this shortly bends left continue ahead through a boatyard complex along the approach road to Brixedone Farm, curving right en route to pass under the M27.

Just short of the farm, cross a stile on your right to follow a meadow path parallel with the river for a short distance but soon bearing left to cross a stile and a footbridge over a tidal creek. Here you enter Upper Hamble Country Park, an expanse of riverside woodland and farmland carefully managed for conservation coupled with public enjoyment of a very beautiful and peaceful oasis of unspoilt rurality.

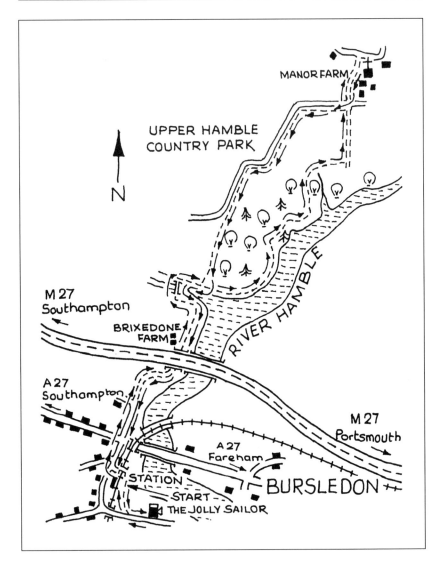

Bear right to follow a hard-surfaced footpath alongside the creek and then once again parallel with the Hamble River estuary, viewed through a screen of trees to your right. A stepped path soon leads right-handed to a pontoon, located close to the sunken wreck of what is thought to have been Henry V's great warship the *Grace Dieu*, struck by lightning and destroyed by fire in 1439. A waterside path leads you on from here to rejoin the main path, from which another subsidiary path soon diverges right to the river bank again. From this point on keep as close to the river as paths permit, with a fence on your right-hand side, until you reach a crossing of paths where the fence and its accompanying path bend sharply right, downhill towards the river. Follow this path to its end.

A gravelled path now leads you on through the wood to a point at which it bends left but you continue right-ahead along a stepped path which descends to a stream footbridge, then climbs to a cycle-barrier where you leave the wood and follow the leftward edge of a field which dips to the river on your right.

Your path soon turns left through a gate to follow a farm track towards Botley Manor Farm, owned and maintained with its old outbuildings by Hampshire County Council as 'a working farm from a bygone age'. The farm is open daily from 10 am to 5 pm between Easter and 31 October, and from 10 am until dusk on winter Sundays and during the school half-term holiday week in February. Just beyond the farm and its duckpond Botley Old Church peeps out through the trees. This is a preserved portion of the original church of St Bartholomew which served the village, now a mile distant, until the 1830s, when another church was built much more centrally. Occasional services are still held in the older church, which is frequently open to visitors and contains a fine example of an old-time horsedrawn hearse.

Return past Manor Farm and its tearoom to the car park entrance, and here turn right to follow a gravelled track directly alongside a hedged lane which you might not recognise as a Roman road. Where the gravelled way presently turns left continue ahead, still on gravel and with the hedged lane still beside you. Beyond the lane is a small wood where charcoal-burning kilns are present.

Just past a wayside car park you enter woodland, following a hard path signposted at first as leading to a picnicking area and toilets. Disregard side-turnings and continue ahead through the wood to a path-junction by the creek at its far end. Here you rejoin your outward route, which you follow back to Bursledon by way of the meadow path to Brixedone farm, reached by turning right and then left across the footbridge at the head of the tidal creek.

WALK 17

CALSHOT AND SOUTHAMPTON WATER

An old tide-mill and a quiet coast where seabirds congregate survive along this stretch of Southampton Water's western shoreline, made accessible by a footpath many walkers have overlooked. Here is salt water a-plenty and bracing sea air to invigorate you. Sorry about the power station – but we all need electricity!

The old tide mill on Ashlett Creek

This quiet southerly end of the Waterside, as the area fringing Southampton Water from Totton to Calshot is locally known, is steeped in history, ancient and modern. Fawley and its church date back at least to Norman times, the present church having been rebuilt after being bombed in the last war. Oil came to Fawley after World War I, at first in a fairly small way to service ocean liners newly converted from coal-burning to oil. The huge Esso Refinery complex took over after World War II and mopped up much of the remaining unspoilt countryside between Fawley and Hythe. To the south, however, there is a fascinating 2-mile stretch of shoreline which by great good fortune is brought within reach of all by a public footpath. Calshot, at the far end, is one of those coastal locations where Henry VIII had a castle built to protect his realm against invasion after his rift with the Roman Catholics. Throughout much of the 20th century it had a defensive role of another kind through its links with aviation – the Royal Flying Corps, the Royal Naval Air Service and the Royal Air Force all having been involved at different stages. Calshot's more recent function has been to serve as a centre for ground and water-based sporting activities.

Ashlett, where this walk starts, lies at the end of a country lane just over ½ mile from Fawley. Here at the head of Ashlett Creek is a former tide-mill, where corn was ground by power from the outflow of tidal water from a large mill-pond now maintained as a bird sanctuary. By 1890 the mill had ceased to operate but the building has been preserved to become, in our own time, social club premises for employees at Fawley Refinery. A matter of yards away is a pub with as maritime a flavour throughout as one could wish for in such a setting, and yachting folk whose craft come into the creek at high tide are regulars. Opening times at the Jolly Sailor are 11 am to 2.30 pm and 6 pm to 11 pm on Mondays to Thursdays, 11 am to 11 pm on Fridays and Saturdays and 12 noon to 10.30 pm on Sundays. Brews on tap include well-tried favourites such as Old Baily, Boddingtons, Flowers Original, Spitfire and Wadworth 6X, as well as Guinness, Murphy's Irish stout and Heineken and Stella lagers. Food may be ordered from 12 noon to 2 pm and in the evening from 7 pm to 9 pm except on Sundays and Mondays. Seafood looms large on the menu and you will find a good range of starters, meat and vegetarian dishes alongside soup of the day and snacks. There is also a separate restaurant area for which bookings can be taken.

Telephone: 01703 891305.

- **HOW TO GET THERE:** Leave the M27 at junction 2 or the A35 at the western end of Totton's southern bypass to follow the A326 to Fawley, heading as if for Fawley Refinery itself before turning right a little way short of Fawley church into Fawley village. Just past a

79

row of shops on your left turn left to follow the downhill lane to Ashlett.

Solent Blue Line buses serve the area and walkers arriving by bus can start the walk at Calshot Beach or, by adding 1 ½ miles to the total walking distance, from Fawley Square instead of from Ashlett.

- **PARKING:** There is a free car parking area at Ashlett, and walkers using the Jolly Sailor can leave their cars in the pub car park.
- **LENGTH OF THE WALK:** 4 miles. Map: OS Outdoor Leisure 22 New Forest (GR 467032).

THE WALK

With Ashlett Creek and the tide-mill on your left, walk to the end of the car park area where, directly beyond a pedestrian access gate, you turn left to follow a shore-edge footpath. This skirts left of the Esso sailing club premises, with tidal saltmarsh and Southampton Water itself on your left-hand side. The path soon curves right with the shoreline to join a hard-surfaced footpath flanked by bushes.

Follow this path left-handed, with fenced ground on your right for much of its length and, once you are clear of bordering bushes, either a wide expanse of saltmarsh and tidal creeks or the sea itself directly to your left, depending on the state of the tide. High water is perhaps the best time to choose for a walk like this one. When I last walked this way the tide was all but lapping the path in places, and migrant brent geese from Siberia were cruising offshore in their multitudes all the way along to Calshot.

Fawley Power Station with its dominating chimney looms ever closer. Halfway to Calshot your path skirts left of it, crossing as it does so a channel of water by a bridge with a gate at each end. We found the latch on the first gate stiff due to the gate having dropped on its hinges. The power station passes from view as you continue ahead to Calshot, with a firm path underfoot all the way and sea or saltmarsh still alongside you.

At Calshot follow the shore road right-handed, with beach chalets between yourself and the shingly shore to your left – a popular venue on warm summer days, when the beach cafés do a roaring trade. Follow the road where it bends right-handed, heading inland through the village, which mainly consists of

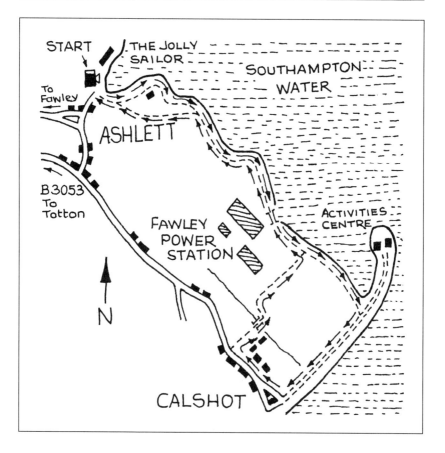

former married quarters for Service personnel and their families. On your left is a pub called the Flying Boat, a reminder of the times when these and seaplanes were part of everyday life here. In a dip at the end of the village a footpath sign points your way right-handed along a shallow vale bordered by bushes. After bridging a small stream, your path turns left towards Fawley Power Station, the security fence of which it then follows right-handed back to the edge of Southampton Water.

Here you rejoin your original path, which you follow left-handed back to Ashlett, enjoying a second bite at the cherry of this splendid shoreline walk. As you approach Ashlett, you can keep to the hard path if you want to head straight back to your car.

81

THE BEAULIEU RIVER AND BUCKLERS HARD

Beaulieu was not so-named, as 'the beautiful place', without justification. Scenic charm of a very high order extends all the way to the 18th-century time-warp of Bucklers Hard along this field-and-woodland walk beside the winding estuary.

The Wine Press at the Montagu Arms in Beaulieu

One of my favourite waterside walks is this one, where pastures, trees and tidal water merge their individual charms to provide a potent mixture of scenic delights throughout the route. Beaulieu itself has an extra special magic. Ever since King John made a gift of the manor to the Cistercian monks way back in the 13th century, it has been very much a place apart from the outside world. Today, of course, it is best known as the home of the National Motor Museum, but people still flock to Beaulieu to enjoy its old-world beauty and the peace of its surroundings between the New Forest and the sea.

The growing of grapes to make wine here traces its origins back to the time of the monks and continues to flourish today. It explains why the pub at the Montagu Arms Hotel, which has been the village inn a good deal longer than anyone locally can remember, is called the Wine Press. Open on weekdays from 10.30 am to 11.30 pm and on Sundays from 12 noon to 10.30 pm, this offers a range of popular brews including Ringwood Fortyniner, Wadworth 6X, Flowers Original, Boddingtons, draught Guinness and Murphy's Irish stout, Heineken and Stella lagers and, for cider drinkers, Strongbow and Scrumpy Jack. Food is served from 12 noon to 2 pm and 6.30 pm to 9.30 pm and includes a good selection of filled baguettes, ploughman's, light bites, starters and salads as well as steaks, poultry, fish dishes and classics such as steak and kidney pie – not forgetting vegetarian specials. Leadlight windows and tasteful furnishings link quality with comfort. Telephone: 01590 612324.

- **HOW TO GET THERE:** Beaulieu lies midway between Hythe and Lymington at the junction of the B3054, between these two places, with the B3056, from Lyndhurst. To reach it from the M27 leave the motorway at junction 2 to follow the A326 to the roundabout at Dibden Purlieu, from which you follow the B3054 to Beaulieu.

  Wilts & Dorset buses operate in the area on weekdays and on Sundays Stagecoach Hampshire buses run at 2-hourly intervals throughout the day.

- **PARKING:** No facilities are available at the Montagu Arms Hotel. There is a free public car park in Beaulieu but this is often full at peak times for visitors. Limited free parking space is available in Beaulieu's one-way High Street and, with permission, at Beaulieu Garden Centre, off the High Street.

- **LENGTH OF THE WALK:** 5 miles. Map: OS Outdoor Leisure 22 New Forest (GR 386021).

THE WALK

Leave Beaulieu car park by the gravelled pedestrian exit to the High Street. At the bottom, to your left, is the Montagu Arms Hotel. After your visit there, head back up the High Street. Opposite the car park exit turn left to follow a public footpath between houses, leading to a stile beyond which you cross a playing-field to another stile, then follow a gravel road right-handed.

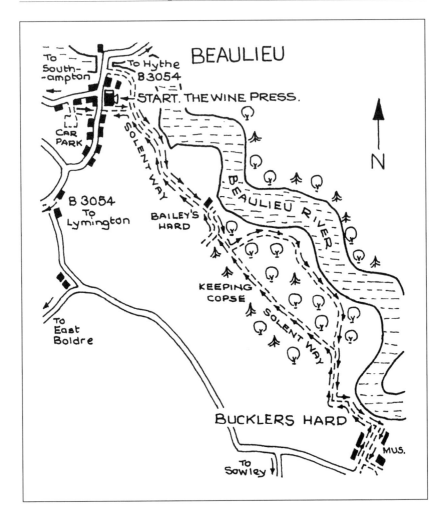

A padlocked gate just ahead is flanked by a further stile, beyond which the gravelled way leads on between fenced pastures before turning left into a field. The Beaulieu River estuary loops between farmland and trees to your left as you carry straight on along a fenced track, soon passing through a finger of woodland bordering a tidal creek. Here you enter North Solent Nature Reserve and continue along a field-edge to Bailey's Hard, where you pass on your left a cottage near what used to be the brickworks for Beaulieu Manor.

Here you join and follow right-handed for a few yards a gravel approach-road, then turn left from this along a hard track into a wood called Keeping Copse. Not far ahead you will pass on your left a woodland track marked 'private', almost immediately beyond which you turn left to follow a well-used path towards the river. Now, for about a mile, your new path follows the twists and turns of a tideway flanked by woodland on both banks.

Soft going in places can be bypassed and at one point I had to jump a narrow ditch to avoid deviating from the path nearest to the river. Eventually you rejoin the long, straight track with which your twisty and scenic riverside path has been running closely parallel all the way through Keeping Copse. Follow the track left-handed, skirting Bucklers Hard Yacht Harbour and crossing the approach road to it to reach Bucklers Hard itself.

The village street, with its wide grass borders and terraced 18th-century dwellings, rises quite steeply from the river, with the pub and the shop on your right as you climb the street, and the maritime museum at the top, on your left. It must be visually much the same here today as when it was a hive of industry, building those 'wooden walls' with which England defended itself against Napoleon. Still to be seen are the launchways from which men-of-war, when otherwise complete, were towed by rowing-boats to Portsmouth for masts and sails to be fitted and guns installed, ready for action. The museum displays numerous relics of those times, and at the hotel named after him, in the very room where he worked, master builder Henry Adams may still be seen, in effigy, poring over plans of one of his vessels. At peak holiday times you can explore still more of the Beaulieu River estuary by taking advantage of one of the boat trips which then operate between Bucklers Hard and the point where the river joins the Solent. At the Master Builder's House Hotel the Yachtsman's Bar is open all day at the usual hours, weekdays and Sundays, and here, in good weather, you can sit out in the pub garden or on the patio to enjoy a pint before walking back to Beaulieu. Restaurant facilities are also normally available.

Directions for the return walk are straightforward. Head back the same way to Keeping Copse where, instead of following the riverside path for a second time, keep to the direct main track. From where the riverside path rejoins the main track near the far end of the wood, continue ahead past Bailey's Hard to follow your outward route in reverse, and so back to Beaulieu.

THE SOLENT SHORE NEAR PENNINGTON

Where salt was once produced from evaporated sea water is now a wilderness paradise for birds and for walkers who enjoy sea breezes and wide open spaces down by the shore. The Solent sea-wall path on this route provides all of these.

The Solent sea-wall path

Between the ancient town of Lymington and the western end of the Solent is a watery area largely given over to nature conservation, a place where the winning of salt from the sea was once an important industry. Birdlife abounds and includes a number of rare and interesting species which any walker equipped with binoculars stands a very good chance of seeing. The old 'salterns' south of Pennington, just a little way west of Lymington, might easily not be recognised today for what they once were, the enclosures where sea water was evaporated to a point at which the resultant brine could be boiled away, leaving just the salt. This became uneconomic when saltmines in Cheshire were exploited as Britain's main source of the product and the 'salterns' fell into disuse after 1865.

Outgoing salt was checked for tax purposes at the pub still called the Chequers, an attractive, creeper-covered building set back a little from a quiet, tree-bordered byway at Lower Woodside, midway between Pennington and the coast. This 17th-century pub was also ideally located to cater for thirsty salt workers on their way home after their hard day's labours. Today a varied clientele is welcomed from 11 am to 3 pm and 6 pm to 11 pm on Mondays to Fridays, Saturday opening being more flexible. Normal Sunday hours are 12 noon to 10.30 pm but this is liable to variation in winter. Brews on draught include three guest ales as well as Wadworth 6X, Bass, Guinness and Caffrey's Irish ale, not forgetting Heineken and Stella lager and draught cider. Five or six selected white and red wines are served by the glass. Home-cooked food is of excellent quality, very reasonably priced and may be ordered from 12 noon to 2 pm and 7 pm to 10 pm on weekdays and 12 noon to 5 pm and 7 pm to 9.30 pm on Sundays – except possibly in winter when Sunday opening hours may be restricted. The bar and restaurant menus are changed regularly and include seasonal favourites, with fish dishes always prominent among the varied choice available. Typical bar menu items are garlic bread with cheese or paté, scampi with chips and salad, and lamb curry. From the restaurant menu you might choose whole grilled Dover sole, half of a local lobster with salad, or cod fillets with cheese and lettuce salad, or you may prefer, say, breast of chicken with Stilton sauce, lamb steak with orange and ginger sauce, or rump or sirloin steak cooked to your liking. Sandwiches, soup and other snack items are also available, and parties of walkers can be catered for with advance notice. As well as the separate restaurant area there is a pub patio and garden, and the general character and décor of the pub are traditional.

Telephone: 01590 673415.

- **HOW TO GET THERE:** From Lymington follow the A337, the Christchurch road, ½ mile west to Pennington Cross roundabout, where you take the first exit (ie the third exit if approaching from the Christchurch direction), signposted to Lower Pennington, then almost immediately turn left from this to follow Ridgeway Lane. This soon leads into Lower Woodside, where the Chequers is on your right.

Frequent trains between Bournemouth, Southampton, Winchester and London connect at Brockenhurst with trains to and from Lymington (Lymington Town station) at ½ hourly intervals on weekdays and hourly on Sundays. Wilts & Dorset buses also provide a comprehensive service.

- **PARKING:** Walkers using the Chequers may leave their cars in the pub car park, and there is limited roadside parking space nearby.
- **LENGTH OF THE WALK:** 3 miles. Map: OS Outdoor Leisure 22 New Forest (GR 322935).

THE WALK

From the Chequers continue along the quiet, tree-lined lane which passes it. As a road for motor traffic this soon reaches a blind end by some fairly isolated cottages but a hard-surfaced, tree-shaded path continues, skirting left of a small lake where swans are often present.

The path leads to another lane, and as you follow this left-handed it soon bends right, with the level expanse of Pennington Marshes extending to your left as you approach another blind road end. Here turn left to follow a straight gravel track across the marshes. One stretch of this track we found to be flooded but this was bypassed by a parallel track which took us dryshod to the Solent sea wall. Raised high enough to protect the fresh-water marsh from tidal inundation, this is topped by a gravel path which you follow left-handed, pausing whenever you feel inclined to cast your eye across the seaway to where the Isle of Wight looms closely.

Beyond sheltered water and spreading saltmarsh to your rear stretches the shingle spit at the end of which is Henry VIII's Hurst Castle, an enduring reminder of measures taken many centuries ago to guard this country against foreign foes. To your left extends that wilderness mosaic of land and water where the salterns used to be and where wetland birds now reign supreme. Very conspicuous among these, when we passed in early spring, was a little egret, a miniature, snowy-white relative of the heron, new to Britain, and a little way farther on we saw a second of the species.

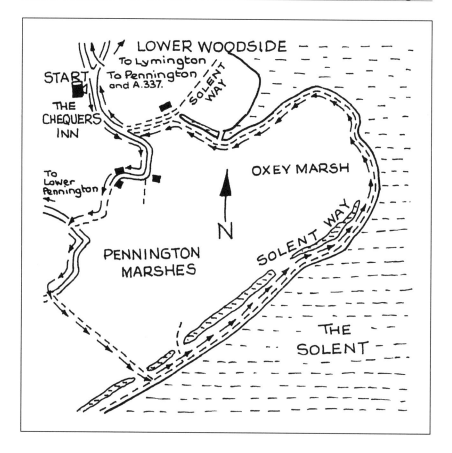

As it follows bends in the sea wall, your path encompasses Oxey Marsh before turing left, with a creek alongside it and the Solent proper now behind you. The creek narrows as you approach a substantial sluice-gate, which is crossed in its turn by a path. Disregard this and keep straight on, down some steps with a channel of water still to your right. Your path skirts left of a house at the head of this channel and duplicates itself to offer two parallel routes back to the lane you took south from the Chequers pub at Lower Woodside, and which you now follow in reverse.

RINGWOOD AND THE AVON VALLEY PATH

Hampshire's mightiest river loops its leisurely way between lush pastures where wildflowers flourish in their multitudes each spring. This walk along watermeadow paths and quiet lanes to the south of the ancient country town of Ringwood is highly recommended.

The Original White Hart at Ringwood

This walk from Ringwood, near the New Forest's western border, is a very special one. It provides a close encounter with a chalk stream fuller-bodied than either the Itchen or the Test – the so-called Hampshire Avon, which rises in Wiltshire and ends in Dorset, collecting several other fairly substantial rivers on the way – and includes a stretch of the Avon Valley Path, the long distance route between Salisbury and Christchurch. This passes through Ringwood town centre, where you join it at the start of the walk.

The Forest is close enough for a lucky white hart, or stag, supposedly to have ended up with a charmed life and a crown of gold around its neck as a special mark of royal favour after being hunted by Henry VII and his courtiers. Having been released for the hunt, the hart was recaptured after refusing to run any further when it reached the watermeadows near Ringwood, but in the meantime it had given such an exceptionally good day's sport that it was honoured by the King in the manner described, or so runs the legend. A further embellishment has the monarch and his companions later repairing for refreshment to the Ringwood inn which has claimed ever since to be 'The Original White Hart', taking its name from that day's events.

The inn, in the High Street, is so old that efforts to ascertain its actual age have so far proved unsuccessful, but it seems there may have been a hostelry on the same site in the 12th century. There are no doubts whatsoever that it was once an important posting-house where stagecoaches changed their horses and passengers on long journeys stopped off for food and accommodation. Open all day from 10 am to 11 pm (12 noon to 10.30 pm on Sundays), with its ancient beams, low ceilings and two inglenook fireplaces, along with other period features, this Eldridge Pope house is a traditional pub in almost every aspect. Ales on tap include Hardy Country, Pope's and Royal Oak, with Carlsberg and Kronenbourg lagers, Guinness and Blackthorn cider also on draught. Food is served from 12 noon to 2.30 pm and 6.30 pm to 9.30 pm, except on Sunday evenings, with a menu ranging from bar snacks to full-blown restaurant meals, and everything is home-cooked. You can fortify yourself before or after the walk with items like vegetable tikka masala, beef and mushroom pie and bacon and liver casserole, while those in a hurry may opt for sandwiches, toasties or ploughman's. You may be tempted by a traditional Sunday lunch on the day in question, to enjoy in the bar or in the restaurant, according to your preference, and there is a separate eating area for non-smokers – and a large rear patio for fine summer weather. Families with children are welcome.

Telephone: 01425 472702 or 473313.

- **HOW TO GET THERE:** Ringwood lies just off the A31, 11½ miles south-west of Cadnam, where the M27 has its western end, and the town is also reached by the A338 from both Salisbury and Bournemouth. Head for the long stay car park (see parking details), plainly signposted on entering the town.

  Ringwood is served by Wilts & Dorset buses, Solent Blue Line and Stagecoach Hampshire buses. There are also various local bus services.

- **PARKING:** The walk starts from Ringwood's large, free Central Car Park, clearly signposted. This is situated in Stallard's Lane. Choose the long stay car park, use of the short stay one being limited to two hours. The White Hart's rear car park may be available to walkers who first obtain permission, but not at busy times.

- **LENGTH OF THE WALK:** 4½ miles. Map: OS Outdoor Leisure 22 New Forest (GR 147054).

THE WALK

With the tower of Ringwood's parish church looming a short distance to your right, follow the road past the short stay car park towards the town centre, then turn right along narrow Meeting House Lane. This brings you to Ringwood High Street, where The Original White Hart, on your right, is just one of many period buildings.

Carry on past the old Market Place, faced on your right by the 19th-century church of St Peter and St Paul. This replaced a church which dated in part from the 13th century. Now continue past the Red Lion Hotel along West Street where, on your right, before bridging an arm of the Avon on the western outskirts of Ringwood, you pass a particularly lovely old thatched and timber-framed cottage which now functions as a restaurant.

Directly after crossing the river, below where two scenic channels converge around a public open space with riverside seating, turn left along a road which leads you through a residential caravan park. By a footpath sign and a stile at the end of this you enter a meadow, across which your path angles slightly left, back towards the river you recently crossed, and which you here cross again by a footbridge. Not many yards further on you join and follow right-handed a road flanked on both sides by houses, with an intervening green. Where the houses end turn right to follow a gravel road which bridges the

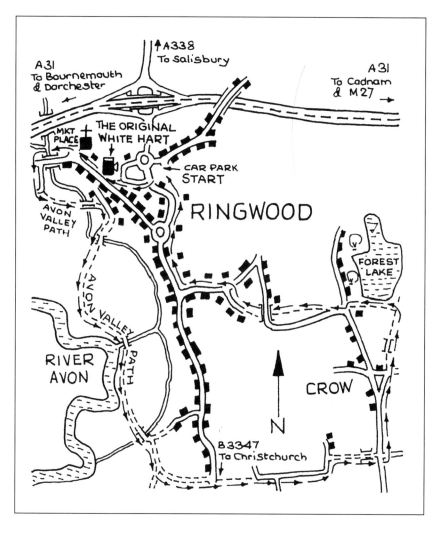

river at a spot much favoured by youthful anglers. You then cross the course of what used to be the Southampton-Dorchester railway, routed via Ringwood instead of Bournemouth because, when the line was constructed, the seaside resort did not yet exist. All trains of course now run via Bournemouth, the 'old road', as railwaymen called it, having been closed in the 1960s.

A stile now precedes a moist meadow, where a boardwalk eases your way across the wettest stretch to another stile. Here you enter a large, level pasture, spreading away, as it seems, to a

93

A charming thatched cottage, south of Ringwood

far horizon where trees line a long, low ridge on the western side of the Avon Valley. On a sunny May day I found this pasture smothered in spring flowers, with the yellow of kingcups and dandelions merging into a sea of white where they intermingled with cuckoo flowers – what some of us used to call milkmaids and botanists know as the greater stitchwort. Environmentally friendly farming has helped preserve this springtime magic.

A fence at first flanks your path on the left. Where the fence soon bends away to your left you carry straight on across the pasture, the route being plainly evident. The path itself presently angles slightly left to converge with the main channel of the Avon where this winds unhurriedly and voluminously between riverside watermeadows. I have seen swans and a Canada goose before and after crossing a footbridge where a small side-channel joins the main river.

After keeping close company for a short distance, path and river separate as you now head towards a stile, from which point your path becomes a fenced green lane. This leads to a ford parallel with a footbridge where you cross once again the lesser arm of the Avon which you first encountered as you left Ringwood. A secondary footbridge alongside a muddy farm track takes you left-handed for a few yards to a point near the end of a metalled road, where you turn right to follow a gravel lane. Where this soon divides you leave the Avon Valley Path to follow a left-turning gravel lane. Flanked by trees which encircle a sizeable lake on your right, this lane leads you to the Ringwood–Christchurch road, which you cross straight over to follow a signposted footpath along the right-hand edge of an unfenced margin between two fields.

This path emerges by way of a farm track onto a very narrow lane. Follow this right-ahead to where it very soon bends right and you follow Green Lane – a metalled byway – straight ahead. Just past where this soon bends left, a green 'right of way' flanked by trees and hedges leads you right-handed, bridging a roadside brook where it joins a lane which you follow to the left.

Beyond cottages on your left you take a narrow, right-forking lane. Within a very short distance this joins another lane, on the far side of which a stile precedes a footpath along the left-hand edge of a paddock. On your left is a brook, which you cross by a footbridge preceded by a second stile. With the brook now on your right, you approach and cross a third stile and then go over the course of the old railway again.

Turn left now to follow a footpath separated by a fence from Forest Lake, on your right – an extensive one-time gravel working now fringed by trees and often raucous with the honking of large numbers of Canada geese. Where the lake ends a stile precedes two paddocks, emerging from the second of which across another stile you reach and cross a road to follow, for a few yards, Crow Arch Lane before turning right to take a path along the course of the old railway. Fields flank your approach to Crow Arch itself, after passing through which your path emerges past derelict industrial land onto a road called Embankment Way. This leads ahead to Castleman Way, which you follow left-handed to Christchurch Road. Bear right to follow this into Ringwood, where Mansfield Road soon leads you right-handed back to the Central Car Park. Christchurch Road itself leads on to join High Street, where the White Hart pub is on your right.

Information

LIST OF BUS OPERATORS

Bus services and timetables are liable to alteration at short notice and walkers are advised to check details with the operators concerned when planning a particular outing.

Mervyn's Coaches, Micheldever
Tel. 01962 774574

Oakley Coaches, Oakley
Tel. 01256 780731/781639

People's Provincial Buses
Tel. 01329 232208 (Fareham); Tel. 01705 650967 (Portsmouth)

Solent Blue Line, Southampton
Tel. 01703 226235

Southampton Citybus, Southampton
Tel. 01703 224854

Stagecoach Hampshire Bus, Basingstoke
Tel. 01256 464501

Wilts & Dorset Bus Company Limited
Tel. 01722 336855 (Salisbury); Tel. 01202 673555 (Poole)